Learning Disability: An Educational Adventure

Learning Disability:
An Educational Adventure

The 1967 Kappa Delta Pi Lecture

by Newell C. Kephart

Achievement Center for Children
Purdue University
Lafayette, Indiana

Published by Kappa Delta Pi Press
West Lafayette, Indiana

Order from:
The Interstate
Printers & Publishers, Inc.
Danville, Ill. 61832

LEARNING DISABILITY: AN EDUCATIONAL ADVENTURE

Library of Congress catalog card number: 68-16104

Printed in the United States of America

Preface

THERE WAS A TIME when it was generally agreed that man proposes but heredity disposes. Highly deviant behavior or personality had to be accepted with resignation, or, if evil spirits were suspected, rites of exorcism were instituted. Mentally ill, backward, brain-injured children were regarded as afflictions not to be cured but endured.

Today we are inclined to say that heredity proposes and that education disposes, or if this is an inaccurate way of putting it, that heredity proposes limits but education really decides what they shall mean. In no field has this dictum received greater support than in the education of the handicapped child: the brain-injured child, the mentally retarded child, and the slow learner. Although it is rash to speak of cures, hopeless resignation has given place to hard work, understanding, and skill.

Kappa Delta Pi is therefore happy to present the 1968 Biennial Lecture by Professor Newell C. Kephart of Purdue University, renowned as a pioneer and worker in the education of the slow-learning child. The lecture brings together the fruits of his long labors in both the theory and practice. Principles, diagnosis, and treatment flow together in this book as they have in the lecturer's career.

Professor Kephart took his Ph.D. degree in child welfare from the University of Iowa in 1936, and his experience includes being a mental hygienist with the Wayne County Training School and a research analyst for the U.S. Employment Service. After serving in the Navy Bureau of Personnel during the World War II years, he came to Purdue University in 1946, where he has conducted the Achievement Center, a research and therapy center for brain-injured and slow-learning children.

His book, *Slow Learner in the Classroom,* is well known to all workers in the field, and he is editor of a series of volumes on the slow-learning child. Last year (1967) he was awarded the Distinguished Service Award of the Indiana Council on Exceptional Children. For several years, Dr. Kephart maintained and directed the Glen Haven Achievement Camp for Children near Estes Park, Colorado, a school devoted to the training of retarded children and the guidance of their parents.

Harry S. Broudy
Editor, KDP Publications

Contents

Chapter I

The Nature of Learning Disabilities

ALL DURING MY LIFE I knew I had a problem; I just didn't know what the problem was. In 1942, at the age of twenty-nine, I discovered it was connected with my eyes. I was at the Coast Guard Patrol Base in Wilmington, California, and had been given what was, to me at least, a detestable assignment. I had to collate one hundred pages of material. I was given one thousand page ones, one thousand page twos, etc., and had to arrange them into one thousand scripts running from page one to page one hundred. I delayed starting this as I knew it would make me sick. I knew I would have to do a few pages and rest till my nausea went away, then do a few more pages and rest, etc. I went into the mess hall to take advantage of the long tables and, walking along with a stack of page ones in my hand, I placed them one at a time on the table. Within five minutes I was so sick I had to stop. While I was resting, a thought occurred to me. The trouble seemed to come when I took a page from the stack and followed it to the table with my eyes. There was a great confusion, with the room spinning by. I wondered whether, if I placed one page down and then kept my eye on it lying still on the table, and picked up the next sheet and put it in place without looking away from the sheet on the table, it might be more comfortable. It was. The job took a long time, but I did not get sick again."[1]

The man who wrote these words is a highly successful television writer. As his account suggests, however, he suffered until late in

<hr>

[1] Oppenheimer, J., *All About Me*, Available from Achievement Center for Children, Purdue University, Lafayette, Ind.

life from a disruption of processing of visual information which made simple tasks difficult, unpleasant, or sometimes impossible. After visual data entered the central nervous system, they were not well organized to provide an accurate picture of the outside world. The organization was loose, inaccurate, and distorted for him. Furthermore, the visual data were not organized in terms of the kinesthetic data which were being processed by the organism at the same time. As a result, visual data conflicted with kinesthetic data resulting in confusion, inconsistency, and error. The simplest tasks could, at any time, become major problems.

This man's difficulty is representative of problems displayed by many children in our public school system. Either incoming information is disrupted so that it does not hold together, or outgoing responses are disorganized so that the overt response is inappropriate or erroneous. In the case cited, the major disturbance was limited to the visual input avenue. In other cases, the major disturbance may be in the auditory avenue. In still others, the organization of motor output patterns within the central system may be disturbed so that responses to stimuli are disrupted. It is possible that similar disruptions of other senses (taste, smell, and the like) occur but these sense avenues are less significant in the overall behavior of the human organism and consequently disruptions of these minor senses seldom lead to major disturbances. It is the sense avenues, on which we depend for information (vision and audition), as well as the motor system, on which we depend for response, that the problems of these children are most obvious.

The television writer has described for us how such problems can interfere with daily activities of the adult. How much more, however, must they interfere with the learning activities of the child. One of the major aspects of the learning problem is the organization and integration of perceptual and conceptual information. It is this very organization of information, however, which is interfered with by such problems. Information which we assume will come together in organized integrated categories does not do so for these children. Any presentation of information which we make is received by this organism in bits and pieces rather than in total integrated wholes. These bits and pieces remain isolated and do not come together in clusters. The great organizing ability of the central nervous system is disrupted.

Such problems will exist not only on the symbolic level but also on the perceptual and motor levels. As a result, there is continual confusion and conflict between items of learning; the further learning progresses, the greater the confusion and the greater the conflict.

These children have been known to us in the public schools for many years. Only recently, however, have we isolated the nature of their problems and been able to describe it. This group of learners has recently been called children with learning disorders.

Now that the symptoms have been described,[2] it is possible to investigate the incidence of problems of this nature. One survey of a normal school population investigated the incidence of behavioral symptoms characteristic of learning disorders. This survey found that 17 per cent of the normal school population displayed this problem in sufficient degree to cause significant reductions in school achievement or to make such achievement extremely costly to the organism, as in the case of the television writer. A second survey, approaching the problem from the opposite direction and investigating neurological symptoms, found a percentage of 20 to 22 among the normal school population. These two surveys, approaching the problem from opposite directions so to speak, are in major agreement. It would, therefore, appear that problems of learning disorder affect at least 15 to 20 per cent of our school population.

The percentage of children uncovered by these surveys is relatively high. It means that in a typical classroom of 30 children,

---

[2] Clements, S. D., *Minimal Brain Dysfunction in Children,* Public Health Service Publication No. 1415, U.S. Government Printing Office, 1966.

five or six are struggling to achieve academic success in the face of a learning handicap. Five or six children in every classroom find the demands of our curriculum unattainable or, if they can be obtained, it is only at a major expense to the organism in terms of discomfort, fatigue, or in some cases, well-being.

The further learning proceeds, the greater are the demands for organization and integration of the acquired information. The acquisition of reading skill provides an illustration. In the early stages of reading, the child is required to develop a sight vocabulary. To do this, it is only necessary that he recognize certain key perceptual elements within a word. Thus, he may recognize a word by the cross on the t, the dot on the i, the tail on the y, or some other single characteristic of the perceptual configuration. A little later on in the process, however, he will be presented with methods of word analysis. These methods require breaking down the total word into parts, dealing with these parts separately, but never losing the whole and the relationship of the parts within the whole. For this word analysis task, single perceptual characteristics are wholly inadequate. It is now necessary that the child integrate all of the perceptual factors within the word, preserve this integration, manipulate its parts, re-integrate, and respond on the basis of the integration. The early stages of reading put little emphasis on integration and great emphasis on the acquiring of single units of information. The later processes assume units of information and begin to place emphasis on the organization of this information.

What is true of reading is true in general of all subject matter areas. As learning proceeds, emphasis shifts from specific items of information to intricate organization among items of information. All school administrators have been puzzled by the child who begins his school career without incident; achieves well until he reaches the third or fourth grade; and then suddenly begins to fail for no known reason. This sudden, unexplained failure results in frustration for the child, his teacher, his parents, and the school administration. Many of these unexplained failures are due to the existence of learning disorders. As the child moved through the curriculum, more and more emphasis was placed on the organization of learned material. It was this organization, however, which was specifically interfered with by his learning disorder. When the pressures for organization became too great, confusion and failure resulted. The failure was unpredicted because the symptoms of learning disorder were subtle and had not been noticed.

One reason why the symptoms of learning disorder seem to us so subtle is that we have difficulty imagining the condition suggested by the symptom. We have not directly experienced this problem and hence have difficulty recognizing it. When we take a page from a stack and follow it to the table with our eyes, the room does not "go spinning by." We, therefore, have never seen what the television writer has seen. Because we have not seen it, we cannot imagine it and because we cannot imagine it, we have difficulty interpreting his overt behavior (nausea, etc.) in terms of a problem which we cannot conceive. Individual things hold together and form integrated wholes. Because this *always* occurs we cannot imagine how it might be otherwise.

Consider the chair before you. It is really nothing but a few sticks and pieces of wood. You see those sticks and pieces of wood in certain relationships to each other, which relationships form a chair. It is impossible for you to see these items any other way. You cannot see a pile of wood, which is really all that is there. Because you cannot see these perceptual items without their interrelationships, it is difficult or impossible to imagine how this object would look to a child for whom those relationships did not exist or were weak and fleeting. He sees a pile of wood which only with difficulty becomes a chair. You see a chair which can never, except through intellectualization, become a pile of wood. Thus, it is very difficult for the normal individual to appreciate in concrete terms the meaning of the statement in a list of symptoms "lacks

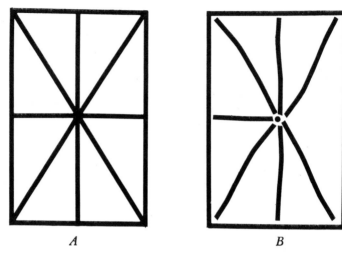

A B

FIGURE 1
Copy of a form by a child with learning disability.

form perception." It is difficult to interpret the overt behavior of the child in terms of this lack of form perception, since we have never really experienced it.

Occasionally, the child shows us how his information lacks organization. Consider Figure 1. On the left is a form which the child is asked to reproduce. On the right is his reproduction of this form. Notice that the internal lines of the rectangle are split. Instead of drawing diagonals across the figure, the child has drawn radiating lines from a central point. If the normal adult looks at this reproduction, he might say to the child "draw the lines straight across" or "it would be easier to draw these lines all at once." Such statements represent a manipulation of the end result of the child's activity. They assume that the perceptual and motor processes in the activity are proceeding in the same sequential manner that the adult's processes proceed. It would not normally occur to the adult that the child does not *see* these lines as diagonals of the figure; that he sees them broken up and disjointed as he has drawn them. Because the adult cannot see what the child sees, he cannot recognize the child's symptoms or interpret his behavior in terms of the basic problem.

It is this difficulty in concretely interpreting the child's problem which makes it so difficult to deal with him in the classroom. These children do not see what we see. They do not hear what we hear. They do not experience from our learning situations what we experience. Because we adults have never been in their situation, we cannot appreciate the confusions and distortions which face them. We fail to recognize how inappropriate relations presented in the classroom can be for children whose experiences differ. These learning situations must be redesigned for such children so that they will convey the information which is being taught in spite of the child's handicap. The learning situation for this child needs to emphasize rather than assume the relationship between the elements present. It should, as far as possible, avoid the area of greatest weakness or, where it cannot be avoided, supplement such information through a simultaneous presentation in another area. These necessary alterations in classroom presentations are difficult for us because we cannot truly appreciate the criteria for such redesign; namely, what the child sees or hears or experiences tactually.

A mother and her ten-year-old son were required to travel 120 miles to meet a clinic appointment. As they were driving down the interstate highway at 70 miles an hour, the youngster suddenly said, "All the cows in that field have a collar like my dog." At 70 miles an hour the mother had only been able to see a herd of cows and was not able to identify any one animal, let alone a specific aspect of any animal. She, therefore, predictably and understandably, delivered to the youngster a discussion on the advisability of differentiating between truth and fancy and not permitting one's imagination to run wild.

Arriving at the clinic, the mother recounted the story of the cows. The clinician suggested that it would be interesting to note what there was about these cows that prompted this response from the child. Therefore, on the return trip, the mother stopped the car at the proper point and carefully inspected the herd of cows. Then she saw that this was a registered herd and each cow wore a leather collar with its pedigree number stamped on it.

Had an incident similar to this one occurred in a school situation, the tendency might have been to commend the youngster for his powers of observation. The excellent visual differentiation would have been noted and the extraordinarily high level of visual performance would have been commented on. Seldom would it have been suspected that the real reason why the child saw the collar was because he was unable to see the cows. To see a cow requires the organization of perceptual elements—horns, legs, tails, etc.— into an integrated whole which represents an animal and in which no part can exist independent of the others. This very dominance of the whole which is characteristic of form perception, however, obscures the details. The normal individual tends to see wholes rather than details because these details are integrated into and subserved by an organized whole. The organization is what is important to us and we overlook the detail in our concern for the whole. Such integration of perceptual elements into a whole was not possible for this child and thus the apparent superiority of visual performance was, in fact, an evidence of a visual-perceptual handicap.

It has proved impossible to teach this child to read. Flash cards, phonics, remedial reading techniques, all have been to no avail. When his response to the cows is seen in the light of an inability to form perceptual wholes and as a weakness in form perception, his difficulties in reading are understandable.

None of us could read if we had to deal only with the details of the print. We read by organized wholes which subsume the details and hence we pay little attention to the nature of the details. The difficulty of proofreading meaningful material illustrates the extent to which we overlook details in the interest of forming meaningful wholes. The youngster described, however, has only details; he has very few wholes with which to deal. It is not surprising, therefore, that reading proved impossible for him. It also becomes logical to suppose that, if his perceptual problem could be relieved, reading might become less difficult.

ETIOLOGY

Since the incidence of learning disorders among school children is so high, the following question arises: What causes these conditions? There are many specific disorders which can give rise to learning problems. However, these specific conditions appear to cluster into three major categories.

Brain Injury. The prototype for the learning disorder syndrome is brain damage. This is the group of children on whom the initial symptomatology was observed and on whom the initial experiments were performed. One of the primary effects of brain injury is the disruption of the organization of behavior both on the input side where information is entering the organism and on the output side where responses to the stimuli are being patterned.

Although the term "brain damage" in its pure sense usually connotes direct destruction of nervous tissue, as in a lesion or concussion, it would appear that other forms of disturbance affect nervous tissue either directly or indirectly and give rise to symptoms of learning disability similar to those of brain injuries of the more restricted type. Included in such a broader classification would be infectious conditions, such as encephalitis and meningitis; toxic conditions such as lead poisoning; oxygen deprivation, such as asphyxiation; and the like. In addition there are conditions which interfere with the development of the central nervous system and result in distortions of this system. These distortions often give rise to symptoms similar to those of brain injury. Thus certain genetic conditions affect adversely the development of the nervous system, or interfere with the chemistry of the body in such a way that the functioning of nerve cells is retarded.

In these more extensive conditions, where there is interference with the anatomical or physiological function of the central nervous system, the same educational strategies originally developed for the brain injured seem effective. It, therefore, seems logical from an educational point of view to consider such conditions under the classification of brain damage. It should be remembered, however, that this represents an extension of the original classification and that not all cases will respond to the same educational program.

Emotional Disturbance. It seems possible that there are two types of emotional disturbance. The first of these is the traumatic disturbance in which a child encounters an incident which is so highly charged emotionally that his behavior is disrupted. Such a traumatic experience is limited in time but is extremely intense. The effect of such traumatic experiences appears to be to interfere with the behavior, but not to interfere with learning. In the school situation such traumatic emotional disturbances require emotional support in the classroom situation coupled with psychotherapy or similar techniques to relieve the distress.

A second type of emotional disturbance results from experiences which are less highly charged emotionally but are extended over time. These prolonged emotional disturbances result in continued emotional stress to the organism. The result appears to be an adaptation to this stress following Selye's General Adaptation Syndrome. Among the results of such adaptation appears to be an interference with functional relationships within the central nervous system. Thus this prolonged emotional disturbance produces effects very similar to brain injury.

The prolonged emotional disturbance interferes with behavior but it also interferes with learning. This interference with learning is very similar to the interference observed in the brain-damaged child. In the school situation, such children require a modification of teaching techniques very similar to that required by the brain-damaged child.

Experience. At least certain phases of learning are hierarchical in nature. The development of one stage is essential to the development of the next stage. Activities of the second stage are dependent upon adequate performance of activities of the first stage. In certain academic areas we recognize this hierarchical nature of learning. Thus we realize that knowledge of arithmetic is essential to the study of algebra and that algebraic manipulations will be largely impossible without a firm foundation of arithmetical information. We organize our learning experiences in terms of these hierarchical relationships. Such hierarchical relationships in learning exist on the readiness level as well as on the academic level. Certain readiness skills are dependent upon each other in the same way that certain academic skills are dependent upon each other. These readiness skills are in part the result of maturation but they are also in part the result of learning. If the necessary learning experiences in the readiness stage are not presented, the hierarchy of readiness skills may be upset with resulting confusion at the higher levels. For these reasons certain deprivations of experience may lead to learning disabilities. The organization of information is disrupted and in much the same way that it is in the brain-injured child. The disruption in this case, however, is due to inadequate presentation of learning experiences.

It is for this reason that high proportions of learning disorders are being observed among children in Head Start and similar programs for the culturally deprived. It is necessary, however, to distinguish between overall cultural deprivation and specific interference with hierarchical learning. Overall cultural deprivation presents learning situations of all types but does not present enough of any of them. The result is an overall lowering of performance level with the result that problem solving is erroneous because of a general limitation of the data which have gone into the solution.

On the other hand, experiential deprivation may be more intense so that an extreme lack of learning experiences exists in one of the critical hierarchical areas of learning. This latter, more intense deprivation leads not only to a restriction in a performance, but to the disruption in learning behavior as well. Since developmentally earlier stages of learning have not been adequately accomplished, subsequent stages become confused and disturbed. The result is learning behavior very similar to that observed in the brain-injured child.

EDUCATIONAL IMPLICATIONS

The learning disorder is a specific syndrome. It is characterized by a disruption in the processing of information within the central nervous system. It arises from a number of etiological situations. It is most prominently observed in learning situations since a major aspect of learning is organization of material. As such, it is of particular significance to education.

The learning disorder, being a specific syndrome, cuts across many of the established categories of learning difficulty. Thus, depending on the nature and extent of the disturbance, the child may show high intelligence or low intelligence. Learning disorders may be present in children with IQs of 30. They may be equally present in children with IQs of 150. They may exist in children from low social economic homes. They may likewise exist in children from the highest social economic levels of the community. They may manifest themselves in school failure. They may permit academic achievement, but make exorbitant demands on the organism for such achievement. They may be accompanied by major disturbances of conduct. They may be internalized, the child "suffering in silence."

Since the learning disorder is so closely related to the learning function, it becomes a primary problem of education. To meet the needs of these children, the school must learn to design educational presentations with their problems in mind. It has already been pointed out that the basic nature of the syndrome is a disruption in the processing of information and response. The individual symptoms composing the syndrome (distractibility, hyperactivity, perseveration, detailed response, emotional lability, etc.) can all be seen as a specific manifestation of the overall disruption. These children do not spontaneously integrate information and form generalizations as does the child with no learning disorder. It follows that educational presentations must be designed to encourage the development of such generalization to a much greater degree than is necessary with the average child.

It has also been suggested that these learning problems begin early in life. They, therefore, interfere with many of the activities which have been called readiness skills. The child will, therefore, come to the school with learning problems already established. To meet his needs it will be necessary to design school experiences which can provide more intensively for learning at the pre-school or readiness level. The school will, therefore, need to teach readiness rather than assume that the child will come to the classroom with readiness already established.

The child with learning disorders presents an educational challenge. His problems are at the very heart of education and emphasize the basic aspects of learning. Such children exist in our classrooms in sizable numbers. They, therefore, demand that education re-evaluate its procedures and practices and adapt its activities to their requirements. At the same time, the educational demands of these children are not unique. Their learning processes are no different from those of other children; they are merely disrupted. This disruption calls our attention to the fundamental aspects of learning which in the past we have been able primarily to take for granted. What we learn about teaching from their demands will therefore intensify and elaborate our educational service to normal children. A careful study of the educational requirements of the child with learning disorders can thus contribute markedly to excellence in teaching throughout the educational system.

Chapter II

Development and Learning

DEVELOPMENTAL SEQUENCES

T HE MAJOR LEARNING PROBLEM for the human organism is that of coming to some kind of acceptable terms with his environment. He must work out an adjustment which will permit him to live in sufficient harmony with the universe around him so that life can be sustained and basic satisfactions can be obtained. The development of such an adjustment is the initial learning problem of the child and continues with varying degrees of complexity throughout his lifetime. It involves gathering, processing, and storing information about the universe and the relationships which obtain within it. On the side of the organism it involves an understanding of the response capabilities of the organism and how these can be modified or extended to fit the relationships within the environment.

Although the organism comes into its environment with certain built-in responses designed to insure a rudimentary adjustment sufficient to maintain life and provide its most basic satisfactions, the major aspects characteristic of the complex adjustments of the adult are learned. Such learning takes place in terms of a number of encounters between the organism and its environment. As a result of these encounters, information about the environment is generated and is systematically retained in the organism for use in later encounters. The responses of the organism are modified or expanded so that the satisfaction obtained from the encounter is maximized. These modifications of response are also stored systematically within the organism in conjunction with the information available from the encounter. As a result of numerous such experiences, a correlated body of structured information is developed, by which a match is established between environmental information and the most satisfying available response.

Such environmental encounters begin very simply and increase in complexity as the child grows and develops. The organism's responses increase both in extent and complexity. The child develops a series of strategies for handling increasing quantities of outside information per unit of time. Concurrent with these two lines of development an intricate matching procedure between outside information and internal responses is established.

Motor Stage. The child's initial encounters with the universe are motor encounters. The child moves and as a result of this movement an encounter with the environment occurs. Such external encounters at this stage are random and haphazard. The child is concerned with his own movement and with determining the nature and extent of this movement. Attention and concern is directed toward the movement and the results of the movement are secondary.

It is during this stage that the child develops the tools for environmental encounters. He learns what the parts of his body are, what responses they can make, how to produce these movement responses, and how to recognize what response has occurred. He is concerned with determining how and what kind of environmental encounters he can generate through his own movement and his own response.

In this motor stage, the child is in effect learning how to experience his environment. A number of years ago, in elementary education, it used to be said that in the first three grades the child learned to read. In the later grades he read to learn. This was an unfortunate cliché in education and, if it is overworked, it can become unfortunate in describing development. However, if we do not carry it too far it may help us to appreciate the motor stage of development if we say, "during this stage the child is learning how to contact his environment." He must first learn what tools are available to him and how to use them. Later he can apply these tools to the learning of purposeful and extensive environmental interactions. Out of these early motor learnings the child determines how to initiate a contact with the environment and how to control this contact. The first control, therefore, of the environment-organism interaction is a motor control and involves the control of the organism itself. As these motor experiences increase in number and the resulting learnings develop in a sequential fashion (as described below), a body of information is developed. The body of information permits the child voluntarily to initiate and to control the nature and extent of interactions between the organism and the surrounding environment. The result is the establishment of a control over the organismic end of the interaction.

It is probably inaccurate to suppose that all of the activity of this stage in development is purely motor. When the organism moves, certain perceptual information is automatically generated. Thus, in the muscles and joints there are sensitive end organs which are stimulated when movement occurs. It is therefore technically impossible to have movement without a resulting effect. However, the organism is also organized neurologically so that, at the conscious level, any perceptual information can be suppressed. By virtue of the fact that it is not attended to, it has no effect. Although the sensory impulses are received by the cortex, they are not processed and, therefore, behave functionally as though they had not been received in the first place. Such sensory signals will stimulate reflexive behavior, which is largely non-voluntary, but will have little or no effect on voluntary behavior.

The aimless, thrashing behavior of the infant in the crib would suggest that at this stage he is primarily interested in producing movement. Although he is generating a mass of kinesthetic information, he appears not to be attending to these perceptual data and they do not appear to be influencing his behavior. It, therefore, seems possible to assume that the initial response is purely motor.

However, because of the very close and intimate tie between kinesthetic information and movement, the child very early becomes aware of the correlation between these two factors. Because this correlation is so obvious, he quickly moves to the next stage of development and, in the case of kinesthetic and tactual perception, which are on or within the organism itself, there is overlapping or bridging between the purely motor stage of development and the succeeding stage.

Motor-Perceptual Stage. During the initial stage of development the child acquired a body of information. This body of information resulted from his motor experiments and the subsequent contacts with his environment. As development proceeded, the body of information was elaborated and expanded. Since it was acquired in connection with activities which were increasing in skill and in degree of control, it was becoming increasingly systematized and coordinated. The result was a systematic body of motor information.

Beginning slightly later than the initial stage in development but running concomitantly with it was a second factor. Perceptual information was being received by the organism. Patterns of energy emanating from the environment were impinging upon the external sense organs. These external sense organs in turn discharged over the sensory nerves patterns of neurological impulses which were conveyed to the central system.

This perceptual information, however, was initially meaningless. The patterns of neurological impulses delivered to the central system by the sense organs were correlated with patterns of energy emanating from the outside environment. They were not, however, related to anything within the organism and for this reason they could not be used to alter or modify response. Although the perceptual patterns may have shown certain relationships to each other, they showed no relationship to what was going on within the organism. The child, therefore, could observe these perceptual data but he was, as it were, only a bystander who could watch the display but could do nothing about it or make any use of it.

It was soon apparent that certain of the motor responses which he had previously learned were closely associated with certain perceptual patterns or with alterations in perceptual patterns. Since the body of motor information was already beginning to be systematized, these closely correlated perceptual data could be put together according to the same system and thereby become meaningful to the organism. The child then began the long process of matching perceptual data to motor data.

In order for such matching to occur, however, data on both sides of the match must be relatively consistent. As long as either motor data on the one hand or perceptual data on the other are obtained in a random or haphazard fashion there is not sufficient control to permit a satisfactory match to be accomplished.

Consistency of perceptual information is obtained by the control of the external sense organ. We point our eye in the direction of the object about which we wish information. We cock our ear toward the source of the auditory information and away from the sources of background noise and confusion. All of the external sense organs involve a voluntary component which permits us to direct them toward the source of information, thereby maximizing the amount of pertinent information which is received and minimizing the amount of non-pertinent information. In certain sense organs the degree to which this voluntary control is possible is extensive. In other sense organs it is limited.

The sense organ which presents probably the most extensive degree of voluntary control is the eye. The eye moves in an extensive arc within its socket. As the eye moves, one object after another in the outside environment occupies the central place in the visual field and the portion of the field in which maximum information is delivered. Through this voluntary control, we can impose consistency on the visual information received by the organism. We can determine what we will see by determining the direction in which we point our eye.

For the purpose of information gathering, it is important that the child know how to point his eye at the object of interest and hold it there. Such control, however, is learned. We, as adults, know when our eye is pointed in the proper direction because it brings us the information which we desire. Such a control on the basis of the incoming information, however, is dependent upon a systematic body of perceptual information so that we can know what visual information we want and when we are receiving it. We have controlled the visual input when the resulting information fits into the total pattern. The young child, however, does not have this systematic body of visual information and therefore he cannot control his eye on the basis of the information delivered. Because he cannot use information to monitor vision, the eye is out of control and hence delivers random or haphazard information. Because the visual information is inconsistent, it cannot be systematized and a negative cycle develops. Because the eye is out of control a systematic body of perceptual information is impossible. Without such a systematic body of information, the eye cannot be controlled.

Because of this dilemma the child first learns to control his eye by using some function which is already under control as a stabilizer or governor. The most common function is that of the hand. The child, having learned to control the hand in the first stage of development, now moves the hand and teaches the eye to follow this movement, keeping the hand in the center of the visual field at all times. It is thus that eye-hand coordination first develops. The hand leads the eye and provides the control for the perceptual-motor exploration.

What happens with the eye happens with other sensory information as well. Because of the very close tie between motor and kinesthetic information which was discussed earlier, the earliest perceptual-motor match involves movement and kinesthesis. From this beginning, the child forms similar motor-visual matches, similar motor-auditory matches, etc.

This is the motor-perceptual stage of development: Perceptual information is matched to the previously developed motor information. At this stage, however, the motor information is the controlling factor. Motor data are the important information from any experience. Perceptual information is manipulated against these motor data until consistency between the two sources of information is achieved. Thus, the child explores an object with his hand. During this exploration he also explores with his eyes. It is the hand, however, that tells him when the information is adequate and when sufficient information has been obtained. The visual information is controlled by and matched to the previous motor information. Out of many such experiments, a correlation between motor data and perceptual data begins to emerge. The eye now begins to give the same information as the hand. Perceptual explorations begin to be possible and begin to give meaningful information.

Perceptual-Motor Stage. Perceptual exploration is more efficient than motor exploration. One can explore an object much more rapidly by moving his eyes around it than by moving his hand around it. Furthermore, the eye gives a much greater quantity of information per unit of time than the hand gives.

For this reason the child begins to depend more and more upon perceptual explorations. He will explore an object visually and will use his hand only to confirm the visual information or to augment it when for any reason it becomes confused. By virtue of the motor-perceptual learning the eye is now under control and can give, except in very complex situations, systematic information about the object. The child then enters the next phase of development, the perceptual-motor stage.

At this stage the primary information is perceptual. Motor information is used only to confirm or augment. For example, in eye-hand coordination, the eye now leads the hand. The eye performs the exploration and the hand follows along confirming the visual information. The control of the process is in the eye and the major source of information is visual. It is this type of eye-hand relationship which is usually assumed when the problem of eye-hand coordination is discussed. Perceptual information, having been made secondary until consistency could be achieved, now assumes the primary role in the perceptual-motor match.

Perceptual Stage. Perceptions can be manipulated against each other. The perception of one object can be compared with that of another object. From this comparison similarities and differences can be noted and relationships between the two objects can be deduced. Such manipulations can be accomplished without intervening motor manipulation.

Obviously such manipulation of perception against perception is quicker and more efficient than the perceptual-motor investigation which the child has been using. He, therefore, moves on to the next stage of development, the perceptual stage. Here he deals with perceptions in groups. He identifies characteristics of objects through perception and manipulates these characteristics to elaborate an extensive systematized body of information. On the basis of such perceptual manipulations he can predict what will happen in the event of a given response.

The relationships between perceptions exist independent of the response of the organism. Although, normally, the child goes through the process of making these perceptual relationships meaningful in terms of his own response and his own reaction through the perceptual-motor match, it is possible to skip this matching phase. In this event the child learns to manipulate "disembodied" perceptions against each other and builds up a complex fund of perceptual information which he can manipulate skillfully. If we, therefore, ask him a question or give him a task which demands only perceptual manipulation, he impresses us with his ability. If the question involves a motor component, however, the child is in difficulty.

Such a child lives, as it were, in two worlds: a perceptual world in which he sees, hears, tastes, smells, and the like, and a motor world in which he behaves and responds. In each of these worlds he has a mass, a body of information. Each body of information is at least relatively well structured. However, the two bodies of information are not matched. Therefore, he cannot use his perceptual activity to guide or influence behavior or response.

Many children in the schoolroom behave as though their perceptual information and their motor information were not matched. Thus, the child is seen who can match perceptual stimuli and indicate whether they are the same or different. He can identify geometric forms, letters, figures, and the like. However, he cannot reproduce these figures, nor can he create a figure like the one which is presented to him. Sometimes such a child excels in reading but is unable to cope with the problem of writing. If he is presented with a design composed of colored blocks he has difficulty reproducing the design with a similar set of blocks. He can immediately perceive that his production is not like the original. However, when he attempts to improve on it, he encounters difficulty and fails again. It would appear that many of these children have developed a body of perceptual information which they can manipulate with some degree of skill, but have never successfully matched this perceptual information to the previous motor information. Their behavior, therefore, frequently seems not to be pertinent to the information upon which it is based.

It is therefore important that before the child is pressed for perceptual judgments or perceptual manipulations he achieve a systematic control of his perceptual world through the motor-perceptual match and that these perceptual data be meaningful in the determination of behavior through the perceptual-motor match. When the developmental stages outlined previously have been followed in order, such an integration of perceptual and motor information is achieved.

Perceptual-Conceptual Stage. As perceptions are compared with each other, certain similarities appear. These similarities can be collected together and integrated into a new whole. It would appear that the initial concepts formed by the child are the result of these abstracted similarities among perceptions.

Thus, the child has experience with the perceptual object, chair. This initial experience is elaborated by a large number of experiences with similar articles. He has perceptual experiences with hard chairs, soft chairs, wooden chairs, metal chairs, overstuffed chairs, etc. Out of this myriad of perceptions he identifies the common elements. These common elements are brought together and integrated into a new whole. This collection of similarities becomes his concept of a chair. Notice that in the concept no actual elements of perception are present. The concept of a chair is not identical with any chair which has been previously perceived. The concept is an abstraction—an abstraction composed of relationships between perceptions. Thus, the child abstracts the similarities from his many perceptions of a chair. This abstracted group of similarities becomes a sort of "sit-on-able-ness," which represents his concept of a chair. The concept is thus a true abstraction but one which develops out of a large number of perceptions. Thus, perception gives rise to conception.

The concept represents an extremely efficient method of handling information about the environment. Many perceptual experiences can be combined and can be dealt with simultaneously in a single psychological act by using the abstracted concept rather than the initial perceptions. Thus, the abstraction subtends by implication the details of the many perceptions. However, this entire mass of data can be handled simultaneously.

Conceptual Stage. Because of the extreme efficiency of the concept as a method of handling information, the child begins to use this method as soon as enough rudimentary concepts have been developed to make it possible. He thus moves into the conceptual stage of development. In this stage, he manipulates one concept against another. He observes the relationships between concepts as he previously observed the relationships between percepts. Since the concept, at this stage, presupposes the underlying percepts he is in effect observing the relationships between large masses of perceptual information. He thus is able to manipulate large clusters of information against each other with relative ease and can thereby include many more data in the solution of his problems than has been possible previously.

The concept involves not only immediate perceptual information but past perceptual information as well. Since the basis of the concept is an abstraction, it follows that all such information both past and present is integrated and systematized. It is only in so far as such integration is achieved that the abstraction can emerge. Therefore it is clear that information is not dealt with in a random or haphazard fashion but becomes schematized and is dealt with systematically. Not only is past perceptual information implied in the concept but, due to the feedback mechanism, past response information is also implied. This information likewise is schematized and dealt with as organized quantities rather than individual data. In like fashion information not pertinent to the solution of a present problem can be eliminated in organized quantities. In the solution of any problem, large quantities of information can be handled quickly and with a minimum of effort. At the same time the implications of the total body of information are retained.

It is apparent that, beginning with the perceptual stage of development, language provides an important function. The development of form perception involves certain abstractions among perceptual data. Being abstractions, these features of the perception possess no concrete counterpart. They are the result of relationships between concrete elements within the perception. It is easier to deal with these abstractions than with the perceptual elements themselves. In order to do so, however, some ready reference, some single unit is required to help keep them straight and to aid in their ready manipulation. Language serves this purpose. Through the symbolic function of language, a single sign, the word, is attached to the perceptual abstraction. Psychologically these signs can be manipulated more readily than can the abstractions themselves. Since the signs symbolize the abstraction, however, manipulation of the signs yields the same results as manipulation of the perception. Thus, language serves a vital function in the organization and utilization of perceptual information.

Since the concept involves a broader abstraction and a more complex set of relationships than does the perception, it follows that language serves an even more important role in the latter function. Words are assigned to concepts to serve as symbols representing the abstractions underlying the concepts. These symbols can then be manipulated, as would be the abstractions themselves, and with the same results. It is much easier to manipulate symbols than to manipulate the underlying abstractions.

It is apparent that if the manipulation of such language symbols is to be efficient, the abstractions underlying the symbol must be clear-cut and well formed. The importance of the perceptual-motor and the perceptual-conceptual stages is therefore obvious. As in the case of perception, so in the case of concept: the child may achieve the conceptual level without adequate grounding in the perceptual-conceptual level. In this event, the child develops concepts which he manipulates against each other but without reference to the behavior of the organism. Such a child frequently becomes highly verbal. He is able to read or listen to information.

He is able to manipulate the symbols involved in this information against each other readily and extensively. He cannot, however, translate the results of this symbolic manipulation into behavior or response. In the classroom such a child frequently achieves at a high level in textbook material and on textbook tests. When he is asked to apply this information in a laboratory situation, however, he breaks down. It would appear that this distinction between classroom performance and laboratory performance is frequently due to development on the conceptual level without adequate previous foundations in the perceptual and the perceptual-conceptual stages.

Conceptual-Perceptual Stage. As the child develops an increasing number of concepts, he comes to depend more and more extensively on conceptual manipulations of information. He uses perception less and less as a primary source of information and more and more as a confirming function. Just as at an earlier stage, motor responses controlled perceptual responses, so perceptual responses have controlled conceptual responses. A point was reached, however, in the earlier developmental stages where perception took over and provided the control for the motor response. In like manner, at this final stage in development, the concept takes over and controls the percept.

At this stage the concept has the leading role and perceptions are fit into conceptual relations. Thus, perceptions which are incomplete or meager will be distorted or altered to fit the demands of the concepts. Psychologists have said for many years, "We see not what is there, but what we want to see." It is at the conceptual-perceptual stage of development that this statement becomes true. We see not what is there but what our concepts tell us is there. The perceptual information is deleted, augmented, or altered to fit the concept.

Consider the chair in which you are now sitting. Perceptually, this piece of furniture is nothing but a bunch of sticks and some upholstery material. However, none of us can see this bare, unelaborated perception. We see a chair because our concepts have become so important that they turn around and influence our percepts. At this stage, organization is imposed upon the perceptual world prior to the completion of the sensory stimulus. We are able to manipulate via conception such an extensive mass of information that we can predict what will happen. These predictions, because of the great amount of data involved, are sufficiently accurate so that we can safely short-cut the perceptual process and supply from the bank of conceptual information perceptual elements which are missing, unclear, or distorted.

DEVELOPMENTAL PROGRESSION

Normally, the child proceeds through these developmental stages in order, solidifying the activities and generalizations appropriate to each stage before moving on to the next. Sometimes, however, there is an interference with learning which makes it extremely difficult for the child to achieve at a particular stage. Growth, however, does not stop to take account of the learning problem. The demands made upon the child by his organism and particularly the demands made upon him from outside the organism continue to progress as though development had continued. The child then finds himself pressured for performance at the next higher level of development even though the present stage has not been completed. As a result of this pressure, the child finds it necessary to temporize, to behave as though he had progressed to the higher stage. As a result, he begins to deal with the activities and generalizations of the next stage even though the foundation has not been laid in development of the present stage. Since the learnings of each stage are essential to and assumed in the learnings of subsequent stages, confusion develops and difficulties arise which are compounded as time goes on.

Usually these difficulties are manifested by a breakdown in performance at the higher stage. The child finds himself unable to cope with the learnings required. Thus, the child who has difficulty at the perceptual-motor stage will frequently show dysfunction in dealing with perceptual data. He may have difficulty in establishing form perception, figure-ground relationships will be weak and inconsistent, and the relationships between elements in a form will not be apparent to him. As a result he will deal with details of the form rather than with the form as a whole.

Some children, on the other hand, will not show confusion at the higher stage. They will be able to deal with the learnings required at that level. However, to achieve this end, they will permit a break to occur in the developmental process. Thus, they will learn the activities of the higher level without reference to the more basic activities of the lower level. We have seen how children can deal adequately with perceptual data in the absence of a perceptual-motor match. We have also seen how some children can deal (or appear to deal) with conceptual material when the percepts upon which these concepts should be based are disrupted. Such children manifest their difficulties when they attempt to transfer these higher level functions into behaviors or modifications of behaviors. Because of the gap which they have permitted in the developmental sequence, the new learnings remain relatively independent of the old learnings. Since overt motor responses occurred early in the developmental stage, this gap prevents them from translating the more complex manipulations into overt behavior.

In analyzing the problem of any child with learning disorders, it is necessary to determine the point in the developmental sequence where his achievement has broken down. This point of failure will be manifested either by increasing confusion in performances from this point on out or by a lack of integration of subsequent learnings with previous learnings. When this point of breakdown has been identified, therapeutic activities designed to complete and solidify the learning of that developmental level can be prescribed. Therapeutic activities will then be presented level by level from this point to the end of the developmental sequence. By this procedure the child will be picked up at the point of earliest breakdown and carried stage by stage from there to the final conceptual-perceptual stage.

Because so many of the etiological factors resulting in learning disorders occur very early in life, learning difficulties are apt to be manifest at or very soon after birth. For this reason a large number of children with learning disorders will show difficulties at the earliest stage of development, the motor stage, and at all stages thereafter.

It is important to note, however, that this is not always true. The learning difficulty need not always be manifest in the earliest stages of development, but may become apparent only in some later stage. A child may experience developmental breakdown at any stage in the developmental process. Thus, a child may move through the motor stages of development adequately but break down at the perceptual stage. Another child may develop normally until he is asked to deal with concepts. His first learning difficulty may appear at this conceptual level.

The developmental stages are hierarchical. Each stage is essential to the next stage. It would, therefore, be expected that all stages above the point of breakdown would show disruption. The corollary, however, is not true. It is not to be expected that all stages below the point of breakdown will show disruption. We must, therefore, look at the entire developmental sequence when considering the problems of an individual child. When we observe obvious difficulties at one level, such as the conceptual level, we must ask whether these difficulties are due to disruption of some more fundamental developmental process, or whether they are learning difficulties specifically related to conceptual manipulations. In the former event, it will be necessary to restore the developmental sequence before concerning ourselves with the child's conceptual learning. In the latter case, attack on the conceptual problems can begin at once.

RESTORING DEVELOPMENT

Strauss[1] has pointed out that the process of development is unidirectional and irreversible. This means that the child can develop only in one direction: from lower stages to higher stages. He cannot reverse this direction and progress from a higher stage to a lower stage. Neither can he, having reached a higher stage of development, pursue the activities and learnings of a lower stage as though it were his first time through. Whatever he has been able to achieve at the higher level, be it good or bad, now has an effect upon his learning at the lower level. His approach to activities on the lower level and learnings resulting therefrom will be different than they would be had he arrived at this lower level by the normal sequence.

Teachers and therapists alike seem too often to assume that the process of restoring development involves only taking the child back to the level which is disturbed. He is then presented with activities and situations appropriate for a child who has just now achieved this level of development. Because of the irreversibility of the developmental process, the task is not this simple. In the intervening time, interests have changed, interpretations of the environment have changed, learning processes have changed, and compensations for learning difficulties have been developed. The child cannot give up the subsequent learnings and behave as though they had never occurred.

If a ten-year-old boy has begun to deal with concepts yet shows a marked disturbance of the perceptual-motor match, he

---

[1] Strauss, A. A., and N. C., Kephart, *Psychopathology and Education of the Brain Injured Child*. Volume II: *Progress in Theory and Clinic*. New York: Grune and Stratton, 1955, p. 90.

cannot be treated as though he were a normal two-year-old just learning this match. This ten-year-old is in no way, shape, or form like a two-year-old even though his learnings are the same as those required by the two-year-old. The events of the intervening eight years have altered this organism so that learning presentations appropriate for the two-year-old are not now appropriate for him. He cannot forget the past eight years and behave as though they had not occurred. He must be presented, therefore, not with learning activities appropriate for a two-year-old, but with activities designed to teach the same things but taking into account the changes which have occurred in his organism.

Frequently, pressure for performance at a higher level results in disturbed learnings. The child finds it difficult to achieve in the activities of the level being taught. Under the pressure of the demands made upon him, however, he comes to a series of compromises, by which he can perform, but from which he either fails to learn or distorts the learning which he has already achieved. The result is a confused, inconsistent, and inadequate achievement. Such disrupted learning results in constant difficulty for the child.

A twelve-year-old boy in the clinic demonstrated his difficulty in establishing hand-eye control. The eye had never learned to follow the hand. Subsequently, in the school classroom, he had experienced demands for performance in activities requiring eye-hand control. As a result, he made valiant attempts to control the hand with the eye. Because he had never learned to control the eye, through the hand-eye stage of development, the result was a completely chaotic visual performance.

The solution to this child's problem seemed obvious. Since the visual performance was so chaotic, it could do him no good. Therefore, he would be asked to perform blindfolded. When he had learned to reproduce a figure blindfolded through tactual and kinesthetic learning, the blindfold would be removed and he would be asked to match the movement of his eyes to the movement of his hand. He had already demonstrated, through familiar tasks, such as writing his name, that he could perform better when his eyes were closed than when his eyes were opened. It therefore seemed obvious that the removal of vision would permit therapy to move back to the motor-perceptual stage and restore the developmental sequence.

The therapy worked well as long as familiar forms which he had already learned were being used. However, when he was asked to learn a new form by tactual and kinesthetic information, he immediately rebelled with temper tantrums and other evidences of frustration. He could not learn these new forms until the blindfold had been removed and he was permitted to use vision. This occurred even though the vision did in fact detract from his performance and make his productions worse than they were when the blindfold was in place.

Here is a case where the irreversibility of the developmental sequence interfered with the planned therapy. Although, objectively, the introduction of vision seemed to make all tasks more difficult and all learning less certain, the child could not give up the guidance of the hand by the eye, because, for better or for worse, he had learned how to perform at the eye-hand stage. Because vision had come to control the process, even though this control was chaotic, it could not be overlooked or eliminated.

These children, therefore, require educational experiences which are developmentally oriented. When they enter the school system, it is necessary to insure that the required stages of development have been adequately learned. Where they have not, it is necessary to provide specialized learning situations which will aid the child in solidifying these earlier learnings. Such teaching, however, must be designed with the child's present status in mind. Merely recreating learnings appropriate to pre-school ages will not suffice. The teacher needs to understand the developmental progression of children and the importance of these progressions for later learning and achievement. Learning experiences can then be designed which will contribute to present learning by undergirding it with aid in developmentally earlier processes. Too often we have attempted to enrich the child's experience or to compensate for earlier difficulties by simply going back, as though he were chronologically younger, and presenting experiences appropriate to this earlier age. Because of the nature of development, this simple solution frequently proves unsatisfactory.

EDUCATIONAL READINESS

The normal activities of the school curriculum assume that the child has reached at least the perceptual stage of development and usually the perceptual-conceptual stage when he enters the system. Such elementary school activities as coloring, drawing, recognizing differences in forms or letters, etc., assume that development has progressed normally through a major portion of its course. For the normal child such an assumption is logical. For many children, however, it is not. Many children encounter especial difficulty in one or more stages of development because of an interference with this particular type of learning resulting from the disturbance to the functions of the central nervous system.

Where learning is difficult, more intensive and more extensive learning experiences are required for mastery of the skills involved. Unless such additional learning experience is provided, the developmental processes involved in this stage are apt to be inadequately established. Under the normal conditions of our culture, such additional learning experiences are unlikely to occur. The home, the peer group, the neighborhood all assume normal learning and normal development. Therefore, any additional experience which the child might gain from these sources is likely to be a repetition of the experiences which he had in the first place. The intensification of experience necessary to overcome his learning difficulty is seldom provided by such usually adequate sources. Wherever he turns, he finds the learning experiences presented to him to be only minor modifications of those which he has already found inadequate to his needs. Everyone makes the same assumption but, for him, this assumption is invalid.

It is for this reason that the child with learning disorders must turn to the school for help. Only where educators who understand learning problems can alter and intensify learning presentations can he find the help which he needs to complete his development. The educational system must be prepared to depart from customary procedures, which are adequate for 60 per cent of the children, and augment these customary procedures with specialized experiences designed to produce specific developmental learnings. Such alterations are a purely professional task and, where academic learning is affected, are the responsibility of the school.

It will be seen that these developmental considerations are closely related to what has been called in education "readiness." Educators have long been aware that readiness is necessary before basic academic skills can be taught successfully. It has been too frequently assumed, however, that readiness is a product of maturation alone. Maturation is certainly important in readiness but pre-school learnings and other early types of learning are equally important. Because of the tendency to depend upon maturation to explain readiness, the school has often felt that it had only a minor concern with the problem. When a child was discovered who did not display the necessary readiness skills upon entering school, the procedure was frequently to keep him out for a year or so in the hope that readiness would develop. Such delaying of entrance into school, however, had the effect of throwing the child back into the customary learning situations of his home and neighborhood. These customary learning situations, as has been pointed out previously, are not sufficiently intense for the needs of this child.

Therefore, delaying his entry into school frequently did nothing but prolong the problem.

It would seem appropriate, therefore, that the school accept some responsibility for the problem of readiness and begin to teach readiness where it is lacking. As the agency concerned with childhood learning, the school should be prepared to offer the child the intensified learning experiences which he has been unable to obtain elsewhere and by which he can develop readiness. Techniques and procedures for aiding development and readiness are being given increasing attention by research and are described in the literature. Such techniques might well be made a part of the educational process in the school, particularly at the early elementary grades. The school would then be in a position to offer the child the type of learning experience which he cannot obtain anywhere else. At the same time, by solidifying the developmental foundations underlying learning, many later academic problems might be prevented.

The desirability of developmentally-oriented teaching has been discussed in connection with the problems of the child with learning disorders. The importance of the problem, however, is not confined to these more obvious cases. Many children enter school with poor readiness skills. Although, in the normal course of events, they will develop these skills, they will do so with great effort. Time which could have been spent in more advanced learning will be spent instead in attempting to solidify these techniques of learning. For the so-called normal child, therefore, such developmentally-oriented teaching would also seem important. By such attention to his basic learning processes, the school can insure that his academic progress will be as rapid as possible and as efficient as possible. Thus, what we learn from the more difficult problems of the child with learning disorders can be applied with profit to all teaching for all children.

Chapter III

Teaching Generalization

O NE OF THE primary symptoms, if not the primary one, of learning disorders is an interference with the process of integration. It would appear that the integrating process is one of the first to be disturbed when the neurological processes of the organism are interfered with. This disruption of integration is seen in response behavior and in the overt activities of the child. Thus, these children are poorly coordinated motorically, their motor responses are inaccurate and frequently distorted. The interference seems also to be present in perceptual activities. The child behaves as though his perceptual impressions were disorganized. Perceptual elements appear to cling together in wholes less strongly than in the normal child and this child tends to deal constantly with the elements of a stimulus rather than the total stimulus situation. In the more complex processes of conception and symbolic manipulations, the disturbance of integration is also seen. This child tends to respond to details or rote memory items rather than to the total implications of the concept. Throughout all his behavior, this child gives the impression that his world and his responses to it exist in bits and pieces with little connection between them, rather than in clusters of similar items held together in well-knit wholes. He continues to respond to items rather than to situations and his behaviors are specific skills rather than adaptive responses.

It may be profitable to think of this breakdown of integration as a failure in the development of generalizations. It can be seen how generalization would be particularly difficult when the neurological processes are disrupted. The establishment of a generalization requires the simultaneous awareness of a large number of related items and the relationships between these items. Such a complex, multiple awareness must require the patterned firing of a large number of neurones simultaneously. If there is a disturbance, no matter how slight, anywhere in the neural function, it is more probable that it will be involved in such a complex patterned event than in a simple rote memory event.

Furthermore, the most obvious result of such a disturbance would be to disrupt the pattern, since all neurones related to the disturbed neurone would suffer and this effect should fan out in all directions from the seat of the disturbance. The net effect would be to riddle the pattern with non-effective units. Since the pattern depends on the relationships between the units rather than on the units themselves, such riddling would destroy the pattern. As a result, responses dependent on pattern (generalizations) would become difficult or impossible and only behavior based on units would be possible. It is probably in some such manner that the child with learning disorders comes to have so much difficulty with generalization and the development of flexible, adaptive behavior. As a result, learning presentations which we offer him in school frequently do not become basic experiences but remain isolated presentations of data.

In education, the development of generalization has been taken very much for granted. It is assumed that if a child is given basic information, he will organize and categorize this information for himself. Having done so, he will be able to respond on the basis of the principles involved and not be confined to the individual items. Thus, we assume that if the child is taught that $2 + 2 = 4$, he will know that $\dfrac{\begin{array}{r}2\\+2\end{array}}{4}$ or that two plus two equals four. Such more extensive behavior is possible because the child has developed a generalization about arithmetical relationships. It is not possible if he only learns the isolated fact $2 + 2 = 4$ and is unable to relate it to similar numerical experiences. The school assumes that the basic generalization will take place and that the principle will emerge. It is just in the establishment of such a generalization, however, that the child with learning disorders so frequently breaks down.

It is safe to say that for the child whose neurological functioning is intact, the assumption of generalization is a logical one. It is probable that the nervous system is so organized that generalization takes place automatically when sufficient data to permit a generalization are present. It is even probable that generalization is compulsive and that, when the system operates without disturbance, the child can not help generalizing. His generalization may be faulty due to inadequate or improper data, but what data he has will become organized into a generalization in spite of himself.

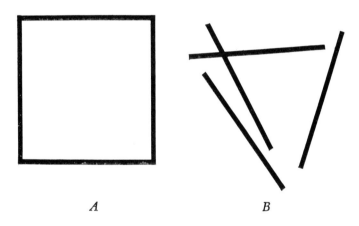

A   *B*

FIGURE 2
Organized vs. unorganized perceptual elements.

Look at the square in Figure 2. Try to see it as merely four lines without any relationship between them. Try to see merely lines without corners or angles or parallelism. For the normal individual such a task is impossible. The figure generalization is compulsive and once the pattern is seen, it cannot be disregarded.

Look at "B" of Figure 2. This figure is truly a random set of lines. It is four lines with no relationship between them. Notice how hard it is to be content with this information. As you look at the figure, now one relationship emerges and now another. None of these relationships are stable because of the nature of the figure but you keep trying. You are uncomfortable with "B" because you cannot develop a generalization to fit it. Your process is such, however, that such perceptual generalizations are compulsive and you must try again and again. You cannot be content with four perceptual elements (lines) which have no relation to each other.

For the majority of the children in the classroom, therefore, the assumption that, given data, they will generalize from them is correct. For those children in the room whose neurological functioning is not so intact, however, this basic assumption of classroom teaching is not valid. They are as content with "B" of Figure 1 as they are with "A" of Figure 1. The relationship between the perceptual units in either figure escapes them. Similarly, facts presented in the classroom remain only isolated facts. Such presentations do not lead to the development of principles because the necessary generalizations do not take place. For such children, it cannot be assumed that the relationships between the items which we present will emerge from a mere presentation of information.

For this group of children, therefore, the school will need to give more attention to the teaching of generalization. This child will need to be taught how to organize material so that the resulting generalizations will emerge. Whereas it has been possible to assume this function in teaching, it will now be necessary to direct special attention to this teaching function for a significant proportion of the school population.

The school has concerned itself traditionally with the teaching of generalization on the symbolic and conceptual level. Our presentations in geometry, science, and the like have been designed to encourage the learning of certain systematic approaches to problems and to aid the child in the establishment of the system. More attention is directed to the system and less attention to the specific illustrations of the system. Such teaching methods, directed toward generalization, need to be intensified and made even more efficient. In addition, they need to be expanded from the symbolic and conceptual field to embrace the development of similar generalizations in the perceptual area and in the motor response area. Little attention has been given in the school to the teaching of generalization on these more basic levels. A number of children, however, come to the school with their most pressing learning needs in precisely this field. To continue with the presentation of information, as though the basic generalizations were being established, results only in increasing confusion for the child and, too often, eventual academic failure. For these children, the school needs to learn how to teach the fundamental process of generalizing as a part of its educational objective.

INITIAL DATUM

In order to understand the principles for teaching generalization it is necessary to consider the manner in which generalizations are developed. The development of a generalization begins with the acquisition of an initial datum. This initial datum is an isolated fact, if we are dealing with a conceptual generalization; it is a perceptual element, if we are dealing with a perceptual generalization; and it is an isolated motor skill, if we are dealing with a motor generalization.

The acquisition of such an isolated datum appears not to be a complex neurological process. Such data can be acquired by a rote process which appears not to involve large masses of neural tissue at one time. It rather appears to depend upon the establishment of a relatively simple circuit from a specific stimulus to a specific response.

It would be expected, therefore, that, unless the particular act involved directly the disturbed portion of the nervous system, there would be little difficulty in establishing such a simple circuit. Observation of children with learning disorders indicates that this assumption is true. They have relatively little difficulty learning isolated facts or isolated responses. In fact, their rote memory is frequently excessively acute and they pick up isolated facts in quantities and with ease.

The first step in the process of generalization, therefore, seldom causes difficulty. The child with learning disorders picks up this initial datum as readily as does the child without such a problem. Teaching this first step does not differ for these children, except that care must be taken to see that the response required is as simple as the datum being taught.

In this connection, it is possible that the techniques of education sometimes hide the child's learning. Thus, in the traditional work-book, the child is often asked to draw a line from an item in a left-hand column to a matching item in a right-hand column. For children with problems in perception it may not be the identification of the item which gives them trouble but rather the process of drawing between items. The latter task is a complex perceptual operation requiring the simultaneous structuring of the page and the two columns of items while the response is being made. Such structuring is particularly difficult when perceptual generalizations are lacking. In this workbook activity, it may not be the datum which is difficult to learn but the process of indicating the learning.

ELABORATION

When the initial datum has been acquired, it is elaborated by the addition of a large number of similar but not identical experiences. This elaboration of the initial datum is the second stage in the development of the generalization. Experiences involved in such elaboration are similar to the initial datum, so that they will be associated and do in fact belong together. On the other hand, they are not identical, so that they will elaborate the initial datum and not simply intensify it. The result is a large cluster of related experiences.

Normally, such elaboration is accomplished through the variation of the initial task. The normal child, presented with any experience, no matter how simple, will introduce many variations into his repetitions of the task. Give him a simple piece of equipment and he will use it in the prescribed manner once or twice. He then starts varying its use. He will do all kinds of things with it—things which are related to the initial use but are not identical with it. These alterations represent variations of the initial task. They are associated with it but not identical to it. The normal child *spontaneously* produces such variations. They are extensive alterations, both in quantity and quality, of the original experience.

It is in this process of elaboration that the first problem in teaching generalization to the child with learning disorders occurs. Whereas the normal child continuously varies his experiences, the child with learning disorders does not. He is content to perform the initial task over and over again in the same way. He repeats the prescribed task in a stereotyped, unvarying manner.

The failure of the child to vary prescribed tasks is probably due to inability to do so. Variations are suggested to the child by virtue of a cluster of information in the central nervous system which is at least partially activated *in toto* as a result of the stimulus. Included in this cluster of information are alternate responses. As this mass of activity in the system is activated, first one response and then another comes to the fore. Since the mass is related, these various responses are associated and none becomes bizarre in relation to the initial task. Thus, the child moves from one response to another as these are suggested by the total mass. The result is a series of variations of the original task: variations, since each is somewhat different; a series, since each is related to the other.

This fluctuation of response within a total mass which is simultaneously active, however, is itself a primitive form of generalization. It is built upon more basic generalizations which have come before and on the beginnings of the generalization pertinent to the present learning area. Thus, the manipulation of objects by the young child, which produces variation in perceptual orientations, is built upon the more basic generalizations of the motor phase of development. This developing generalization, which is the basis of variation, however, is the very thing which the child with learning disorders finds extremely difficult. It is the result of the process which we are trying to teach him. He cannot, therefore, form these variations since they are dependent upon the process which he lacks. He does not vary his performance, because the possible variations are not suggested to him by his disorganized processes of learning. He cannot spontaneously think of any other way to perform the task. No additional methods of response are suggested to him.

Herein lies the first principle of teaching generalization: *The teacher must supply for the child the variations which he is unable to supply for himself.* Since he cannot elaborate the initial datum through variation in performance, such variation must be made a part of the teaching function.

To supply variations of an initial task for the child, however, is not as simple as it sounds. In the first place, such variation requires ingenuity and creativity. These qualities are hard to come by as the time, effort, and money expended by industry in an attempt to develop creativity suggest. A variation means a different way of doing a task. Teachers find it difficult repeatedly to develop unique ways of accomplishing a purpose or undertaking a learning activity. The adult is oriented toward the search for the most efficient method of performing. To alter a procedure just for the sake of alteration is foreign to his thinking.

Furthermore, the child requires not one or two variations but hnudreds of alterations if he is to elaborate the initial datum in the interest of generalization. These variations must be spread widely over all kinds of activities and responses of the organism. It is only through such widespread variation that adequate data for generalization are produced. When the adult has suggested five or six such variations, he has frequently exhausted his repertory since he has learned to see this task in a certain context. It is difficult for him to change context and think of necessary variations in other contexts.

Equal to its difficulty, however, is the significance of creativity and ingenuity in the teaching of the child with learning disorders. As was pointed out previously, the normal child will supply his own creativity if the teacher has difficulty presenting it. Creativity, however, is the specific procedure which the problem child finds most difficult. He has a direct interference with the type of processes which produce creativity. If the teacher is unable to supply it, there is no way this child can develop the variations of performance which he needs. The demand for creativity in teaching is greater with such children than it is in any other area of education. Here is where creativity in teaching is most productive of learning and where its absence is most keenly felt. A teacher assigned to children with learning disorders needs to be the most creative teacher in the system.

There is yet another reason why the development of the necessary variations of performance for these children is so difficult. The teacher has an intact system. For him, items of information come together in logical clusters. Associations between individual items are obvious and unquestioned. Asked to develop a variation on a specific task, this teacher must draw such an alteration out of his own intact system. The child, however, reacts on the basis of a system which is not thus intact. The various items of information or response surrounding the task, for him, are not held together in this logical fashion. This is his problem; this is the result of his failure to generalize.

For this reason, what appears to the teacher as a simple and obvious variation of the basic task may, for the child, appear to have no connection with the basic task. For the child, with his disrupted system, the task and the suggested alteration may have no relationship to each other. The suggestion of the teacher, therefore, does not represent a variation of a task but rather a completely new task. This new task in turn may present as great a difficulty as the initial task since it is not seen as a modification of the original activity.

Figure 3 suggests the nature of the problem. In the left-hand diagram is presented an analogy of the situation in the case of the normal individual with his integrated system. The initial task is represented by the center circle. Alterations are represented by the small numbered circles. These possible alterations are tied to the initial task by the integrating function of the system. The system functions as a whole so that at any time both the task and the variations are present either directly or by implication.

On the right is an analogy of the disrupted system. Here the initial task is related to only two possible variations. Alterations three and four have no relationship to the task or to the variations one and two. These latter experiences are not seen as a part of the situation surrounding the child.

The teacher, operating on the basis of an integrated system, might select alternation four to present to the child. Although for the teacher this is a simple and obvious modification of the task which is at least partially activated already through the operation of the system, for the child it is a completely independent requirement. On the one hand, if the child performs alteration four, it will not contribute to the elaboration of the task since it is not seen as related. On the other hand, the child may find a shift from the task to variation four extremely difficult. When four is within

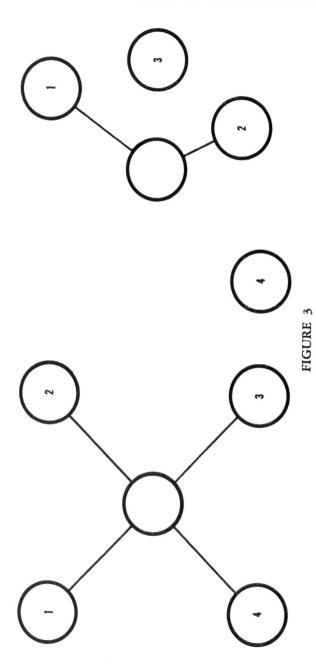

FIGURE 3

Variations of a task depend upon structure of learning

the system, he can move freely to it since he can move wherever he wants within the system and all parts are partially activated. If four is outside the system, however, he has no way to get there. He may, therefore, become frustrated in attempting to "drop what he is doing" and change to the suggested activity.

The teacher has no direct way of knowing where his suggested variation lies with respect to the system of the child. For the adult, it is a minor alteration. For the child it may be an enormous and impossible shift of activity. The teacher's only clue to the nature of his suggested variation for the child comes from the child's behavior. If the child readily moves into the new alteration and behaves as though he were seeing this variation as associated with the initial task, it is probable that the variation is well chosen. If, on the other hand, the child hesitates, shows confusion or difficulty in performing, and behaves as though he were completely changing his response, it is probable that the variation does not represent the same alteration to the child that it does to the teacher. In the latter event, this variation should be dropped and another tried until one is found which appears to be a true elaboration of the initial task for the child.

Teachers of such children must learn to observe the behavior of the child at all times. They must learn to look more at how the child arrives at a response than at the response itself. The important problem is not whether the answer is right or wrong but how the child arrived at the answer. These teachers must learn to observe processes rather than results.

The teacher must also learn to be flexible. Since he can never predict with certainty how an alteration is going to come out, he can never avoid failures in teaching procedures. Neither can he depend upon established methods and techniques described in textbooks to assure success, for the textbook writers are as insecure as he is in any given case. The textbook can only outline the principles. It cannot present the concrete procedure for any given child.

This teacher must expect failure and must be ready to give up what appeared to be a most excellent procedure and try something else at any moment.

Only by such flexibility and such careful observation of what the child is doing with the learning experience presented to him, can the elaboration of an experience in the interest of generalization be assured. If such attention to the problem of generalization is not paramount in the teaching objective, the result will be an accumulation of unrelated facts which, by their very magnitude will increase the confusion and limit the achievement of the child.

The provision of variation in performance is, therefore, a difficult task for the teacher. It is, however, one of the most important aspects of teaching the child with learning disorders. Because of their difficulty in generalizing, these children will be found to gravitate toward rote memory processes in the classroom. Where the other children are varying the tasks and welcoming variations suggested by the teacher, the child with learning disorders will resist such variation and prefer to attempt to solve his problems with ever more complex but unrelated rote memory items. Where variation is implied in the classroom activity, he will take the variation out and reduce the lesson to a rote memory drill. A constant task of the teacher of such children is that of insuring that the child does vary the task and preventing him from developing solutions to problems based on high degrees of skill in rote memory activities. There is a constant battle to avoid skilled response in the interest of generalized solutions to problems. If this battle is not won, the child may learn that $2 + 2 = 4$ with great precision and be able to respond with great speed but not know

that $\begin{array}{r} 2 \\ + \ 2. \\ \hline 4 \end{array}$

Rigidity

When an adequate variation has been selected and presented to the child, it will frequently be found that his response is negative. He does not want anything to do with this new activity and resists the suggestion. This negative attitude toward a suggested task is due to his rigidity.

Rigidity, in the context of education, means the preference of the child for a repetition of a previous activity rather than a change to a new activity. Children with learning disorders will frequently be found to display such rigidity. They prefer to do the same thing over and over. They resist any change of activity and will reject it and continue the old activity. Whereas the normal child will perform a task once or twice and then start introducing variation, these children repeat the original task over and over again. Whereas the normal child quickly becomes bored with a repeated task, these children do not become bored but prefer constant repetition. They tend actively to resist a new task or an alteration of a present task. When a new activity has been learned, they tend to repeat it in the same way, without variation, over and over again.

Such a child was taught to produce a picture of a cat by coloring an entire sheet with crayon, then scratching through the coloring with a stylus so that the color of the paper showed through. The figure which he chose was a somewhat stylized representation but, since he preferred this figure, he was helped to perfect the technique so that the end product was acceptable. When he had completed this task successfully, he immediately set about producing another one. By the end of the week every inch of wall space in the classroom was covered with cats and he was still producing. During this time he resisted any suggestion of change in activity. Furthermore, each of the many cats which he produced was so like the others that it looked like a tracing.

Such is the behavior characteristic of rigidity. It should be pointed out that this boy was completely happy as long as he was drawing cats. He became unhappy only when someone suggested that he alter the activity or the procedure. He did not become bored or discontent and, if he was interrupted, he would voluntarily return to his drawing as soon as the interruption was over.

The child displays rigidity in learning behavior for two reasons. The first of these is due to the disruption of the learning processes. Whereas the normal child has an intact system and can move freely anywhere within this system, this child has a disrupted system which, because of its lack of integration, does not permit him to move. If we refer to Figure 3, it can be seen that, for the normal child, the process of moving from response three to response four requires simply moving through the system from one end point to another. Since the system is intact, such movement is readily accomplished without confusion or disturbance. For the child with learning disorders, however, such movement from one response to another is not free or easy. There is no connection between response three and response four and he has no pathway by which he can move from one to another. Therefore, if he gives up one response (as response three) he has nowhere to go and is left with no possibility of response.

Such a child, therefore, is rigid because he has to be. Whereas the normal child can make rather extensive alterations of behavior without moving outside his already partially activated system, this child cannot move without major disruption. The result is confusion and discomfort. To avoid such confusion, he prefers to repeat the original response and resists any change which would force him away from the very limited sphere which represents all the integrated system he has available at the moment.

The second reason for his rigidity is psychological. He has attempted many tasks. In a large number of these he has failed because of his learning disorder. As a result of these many experiences he has learned that when he undertakes a new task, his probability of failure increases. The obvious way to reduce the probability of failure is to avoid a new task. He, therefore, develops a psychological avoidance of change in the interest of reducing his probability of failure.

Such rigidity directly interferes with learning and with the elaboration of a basic datum in the development of a generalization. Learning takes place only in so far as the child enters into and experiences the learning situation which is presented to him. Rigidity prevents him from entering into any new learning situation and hence prevents him from learning from it. Repetition of the initial task does not result in additional learning. Only in so far as the child alters his response in the light of a new situation does learning occur. Such alteration of response is prevented by his rigidity.

For this reason, it is necessary to overcome the child's rigidity before learning can occur. The child resists the new task because he has to and because he cannot, by himself, move into the new response. He, therefore, needs our help in making such a move. Such help can be supplied directly by demanding performance. Herein lies another principle of teaching for generalization: *The teacher must be prepared for rigidity in the child and must press against this rigidity in the interest of performance and hence learning.*

Pressure against rigidity is applied on three levels each involving, in addition to a demand for performance, an increase in structure of the task. In the first level, it is suggested that the child perform in a new way, "See if you can do it this other way." In the second level, the child is commanded to perform in the new way, "Now do it this way." In the third level, the child is physically guided through the task. The teacher takes his hand and produces with it the movements required.

As has been pointed out earlier, the child fails to alter his performance because he has trouble moving from one response to another. It is to be expected, therefore, that he will resist any suggestion of change and that he will resist pressure against his rigidity. He will be expected to resist with all the behavior at his command. Such resistance may be a passive refusal to do anything at all. It may be an active tantrum behavior in which he screams or physically struggles. Resistant behavior must be anticipated and its nature will be that characteristic of resistance in this child.

There are, however, certain characteristics which are typical of the resistance resulting from rigidity and which make this type of resistance different from other types. In the first place, the resistance characteristic of rigidity is specific. It is a resistance to this task and to this task alone. The child resists the task. He does not resist the teacher, except as he is associated at the moment with the task; he does not resist the classroom situation; he does not resist the surround. His resistance is directed specifically at the assigned task. If he is removed from the task, his resistance vanishes at once. If he is returned to the task, it returns as rapidly as it vanished. His resistant behavior is focused on the immediate task.

The second characteristic lies in the response to the breaking of the rigidity. When the rigidity is broken and the child begins to perform the new task, he behaves as though he had been freed. His response to the pressure against the resistance is a positive one rather than a negative one. For example, one youngster was having trouble in the school's swimming program. He would paddle around at the shallow end of the pool but resisted any suggestion that he get his feet off the bottom. One day when the instructor was convinced that the child had had enough experience with the water to be able to perform and that his behavior was due to rigidity, he grabbed the child and carried him into deep water. Supporting him on top of the water, he ignored the screams of protest and continually commanded swimming movements, saying "Kick your feet, move your arms," etc. When they had proceeded about half way across the pool in this fashion, the child suddenly stopped screaming, turned to the instructor and said, "You know, I *hate* swimming, but this is fun."

When pressure against rigidity has been successful and the child has performed, his response is as though he were grateful for the help in overcoming the rigidity which he could not overcome for himself. It is not that he does not want to perform the new task, it is that his rigidity will not let him. He therefore recognizes when he has been helped out of this predicament.

The third characteristic of rigidity involves the child's response to the newly learned task. When rigidity has been broken and the child has learned to perform in a different way, he embraces this new task with as much enthusiasm as he formerly displayed in resisting it. Thus, he will voluntarily return to the new task and perform it over and over. Once he has learned it, he finds it pleasant and enjoyable.

It is necessary to distinguish between rigidity and perseveration. Perseveration is behavior in which the child gives, in response to a new stimulus, the same response which he gave to a previous stimulus. Perseveration involves a failure to generate a new response. In rigidity, a new response is generated but the child is unable to carry it out. Perseveration has to do with the problem solving, rigidity with the response. Perseveration is attacked through intensification of the stimulus, rigidity through intensification of the response. In perseveration, the stimulus must be manipulated so that a new response is developed. In rigidity, the stimulus is adequate but pressure must be applied to elicit the response.

As was pointed out earlier, the selection of a variation is sometimes difficult. If the variation presented to the child is not carefully selected, it may represent something different to the child than it does to the teacher. Especially in the event of rigidity, this difference may cause trouble. Since this child has difficulty moving from one response to another under any conditions, it follows that this difficulty is greatly increased if the distance between the original activity and the alteration is great.

If the variation selected is a poor one, then a situation is created in which the child *cannot* move from the original response to the new one. With his lack of freedom of movement, it is impossible for him to shift to the suggested task. In this event, if pressure for performance is exerted, frustration results.

Learning does not take place under conditions of frustration. Just as the rigid child cannot participate in the learning situation because he cannot move into it, so the frustrated child cannot participate in the learning situation because, having moved into it, he cannot cope with it. If the problem is rigidity, it can be attacked by pressing for performance. Such pressure helps the child move into the activity. If the problem is frustration, however, such pressure only serves to increase the frustration. Since the child cannot cope with the problem, additional pressure for performance only increases his confusion and further disrupts his behavior. Whereas insistence upon performance is desirable in the case of rigidity, it is contraindicated in the case of frustration.

It is important, therefore, to know when the resistant behavior seen in the child is due to rigidity and when it is due to frustration. As has been pointed out previously, rigid behavior is extremely directed. The resulting resistance is pointed directly at the task. Even though it may be intense, the behavior is narrow. It characterizes only the task behavior not behavior toward the surround.

Frustration behavior, on the other hand, is fractionated. It goes off in all directions and is directed toward anything in the surround or, in some cases, to nothing at all. This behavior lacks any direction or any control. The responses of the child are shattered and cannot be brought to bear on any performance.

In the event of frustration, pressure for performance serves only to increase the frustration and further shatter the behavior. For learning, organization of behavior is required. Hence, under frustration, learning does not take place and anything which increases the frustration, such as pressure for performance, further interferes with the learning.

Therefore, the teacher's response to frustration should be to reduce rather than increase the demands made upon the child. When the behavior of the child indicates that frustration is occurring, the task should be simplified or altered in such a way that the child is able to perform. Only through reduction of the task can frustration be reduced. It is essential to avoid frustration since its effect is not only to reduce learning but, since it feeds upon itself, to further add to the problem so that the effect upon learning is cumulative as the frustration increases.

A word of explanation is necessary concerning the method of reducing task difficulty to relieve frustration. Most teachers think of task difficulty in a normative sense. That is to say, tasks representative of the performance of an eight-year-old are more difficult than those representative of a six-year-old. If, therefore, the teacher wishes to decrease the difficulty of a task, he might drop down from an eight-year task to a six-year task. Such a concept of difficulty of task is based on the over-all performance of children and not on the processes which they use to accomplish the task. It considers only end results, not methods of achieving these ends.

Thus, if a child becomes frustrated in drawing a diamond (a seven-year-old task), the teacher might substitute the task of drawing a square (a four-year-old task). If, however, the child's problem was a perceptual-motor difficulty involving trouble in changing the direction of a line or producing a corner, then the square is little if any less difficult than was the diamond. For children with learning disorders, the difficulty of a task is frequently not related to its normative level but rather to the particular processes required in its performance. Reducing the level of the task for such children, will, therefore, require the elimination or alteration of certain processes rather than a shift in age norm.

It is for this reason that many times the teacher alters the task repeatedly, finally arriving at the point where he cannot think of a simpler task, and still finds the child frustrated. He has altered the level of the task but not the nature of the task. The frustrating feature for the child was not the level of complexity, but one or more aspects of the nature of this task. Care must therefore be taken to insure that, when the task is reduced, this reduction does, in fact, represent a simplification of the task for the child.

When a new variation is presented to the child, therefore, resistant behavior may very likely be induced. This resistance may be due to rigidity or it may be due to frustration. In the former event, the approach to the problem is through the child—exert pressure against the rigidity through demands for performance. In the event of frustration, however, the approach to the problem is through the task—reduce the difficulty of the task for the child so that he is able to cope with it. These two types of resistance can be differentiated by watching the nature of the child's behavior.

This discussion sheds some light upon a conflict which has been apparent in the literature on education of handicapped children for a number of years. One school of thought states that the teacher should press for performance from such children. The opposite school states that, since these children are handicapped already, we should not increase their problems by insisting on performance. They, therefore, council for reducing the stress of the classroom situation.

It would appear that both of these groups might be correct in their recommendations but that they are thinking of two different situations. The first group, which suggests the need for pressure for performance, is possibly thinking of rigidity and its effect upon learning. In the event of such rigidity, they are correct.

If the teacher does not press for performance, he will obtain no interaction of the child with the learning situation and hence no learning.

The second group, who suggest reducing the pressure of the classroom, may be thinking of situations where frustration occurs. In this event, further pressure for performance by the teacher will only increase the frustration and further shatter the behavior. Such shattered behavior prevents the child from effectively entering the learning situation and again prevents learning. For this group, reduction of classroom pressure is to be desired. Thus, both sides of the controversy are correct. In rigidity, no learning occurs without pressure. In frustration, no learning occurs with pressure and pressure only aggravates the situation.

Because classroom tasks are so often selected on the basis of normative information, it frequently occurs that the child with learning disorders finds himself frustrated. If basic processes are disturbed, normative tasks will prove increasingly frustrating since they involve these basic tasks. Thus, the child is presented with repeated failure on a series of tasks, most aspects of which he finds simple, but the final solution to which escapes him. The customary procedures, reduction of complexity level or retention in grade, do not seem to help. He has the same difficulty as before. What he requires is help with basic processes, which is sometimes extremely limited when viewed in terms of the overall demands of the task. Such assistance is seldom forthcoming since alterations of tasks continue to be based on normative information. The result is that the child continues to be frustrated even by conscientious attempts to help him. Thus, the child with learning disorders frequently finds the school classroom a source of continual frustration.

An illustration of this problem is provided by a ten-year-old boy who was referred to the Achievement Center for school failure. Remedial reading techniques and tutorial instruction in school subjects had had no effect. At the time of his referral, demotion to a lower grade was being considered. The clinician discovered that the boy had difficulty with visual fusion. When fatigue developed, the parallelism between the two eyes broke down when the target was within 18 inches and the child saw a double image of the task. The youngster was able to report when he saw such double images but indicated that he had never paid much attention to this fact, since he had always had them and simply assumed that everybody else did too. The result of the visual problem was that, in the process of reading, he would, at unpredictable times see two books before him. His difficulties in reading, especially in rate, now became understandable.

Therapeutic procedures were instituted to produce visual fusion. In the meantime, the child was given a crutch to aid him with his problem. He was told, when he saw two, to close one eye, which gave a single image, until his eyes got back into alignment. Eight weeks later he returned to the Center for follow-up evaluation. In response to the clinician's opening remarks, he pulled from his pocket a tattered report card which had obviously been shown to everyone he knew and which contained all "A's" and "B's." Looking proudly at the clinician, he said, "I'm so glad to know I wasn't just dumb."

This child presented a specific problem in a basic process required by most classroom tasks. Reduction in task difficulty, in the usual sense, through tutorial help and special remedial work, was ineffective, since these alterations of the task left his problem as great as it was before. It would be expected that demotion in grade would have had the same effect. When the basic problem was solved, however, it appeared that the complexity of the task was not the difficulty and performance at grade level became possible. Frequently these children need not so much a reduction in task level as a revision of the task to take account of their basic difficulties with processes. Such reduction in process demands serve to reduce the pressures of the classroom and relieve frustrations where simple reduction of level or quantity of performance do not.

INTEGRATION

When the initial datum has been elaborated through variations of the initial task, the third phase in the development of generalization is reached. This is the phase of integration. Generalization depends upon these elaborations coming together into a cluster. This cluster is organized and integrated into a whole. It is frequently necessary to provide the child with specific aid in the integrative aspect of the development of generalization.

When the central nervous system behaves normally, such integration occurs spontaneously. The organization of the nervous system is such that data related to the initial datum are associated around the initial item as in Figure 3. This entire structure of information is activated in the event of behavior and the response results from the pattern of these inter-connections. When the system is disrupted, however, this disruption destroys the pattern of relationships and prevents their integration into a whole.

Just as the elaboration of the initial datum was facilitated by variation in the information presented to the child, so integration is furthered by the presentation of the same information in different ways. This latter process has been called *redundancy*. Such redundancy involves the simultaneous presentation of identical information in different ways. In such a process, the information is held constant and its presentation is varied. This constancy of the information serves to emphasize the similarity of experience and hence the relationship or integration of experiences.

The most common method of altering the method of presenting information is to change the sense avenue through which it is presented. The three sense avenues most important to education are visual, auditory, and tactual-kinesthetic. Most classroom information is presented to the child through one or a combination of these three senses.

Unfortunately for the child who has difficulty in generalizing, most educational methods concentrate on one type of presentation in any given area. Thus, in reading instruction, the presentation is almost entirely visual. The child is asked to look at a word on a page or on a flash card and call the word. If he has difficulty obtaining information through the visual avenue or if such information does not readily integrate with previous information, no other presentation which might be more effective is offered. For the child whose learning processes are undisturbed, this single avenue of presentation will accomplish its purpose. The visual information will spontaneously become integrated with other information and the desired generalization will occur. For the child whose learning processes are disrupted and for whom visual information alone does not readily provide the basis for integrating a cluster of experiences, sole reliance on vision as an avenue of presentation may result in difficulty and in a rote memory type of response rather than a generalized learning. In the latter event, such a child may, at a later grade level, show a slow, halting reading performance with a lack of comprehension.

In addition to the visual presentation, reading information can also be presented through the tactual-kinesthetic sense avenue. In this event the child is asked to trace with his finger the letters or words as he reads them. In this process tactual-kinesthetic information is either relied upon by the child as the basis of the reading performance or it is added to the visual information to permit interpretation of the written symbol. Verbal or auditory information can also be included by permitting the child to spell the word as he reads it. In this case the auditory interpretation of parts of the symbolic presentation is used as an aid in interpreting the whole. Thus, reading instruction need not be limited to a visual performance but can be expanded to permit more than one method of presenting the basic information. For the child with difficulty in generalization, this redundancy of information may be necessary to produce the integration within the cluster of experiences required to produce a generalized response to the written symbol as opposed to a mere word calling performance.

Recognizing the difficulty which some children have with certain types of presentation, some curriculum designers have undertaken the use of multi-sensory presentations as a basic part of their method. For the most part, however, this use of different sense avenues has involved different information as well. Thus, reading is taught visually, word meaning is taught auditorily, writing is taught kinesthetically, etc. For each area of learning, that sense avenue is chosen which appears to transmit the appropriate information most efficiently.

For the purpose of generalization, however, it is necessary that the information be kept constant. It is necessary that *the same* information be presented by various sense avenues. When the information is varied at the same time that the sense avenue is varied, redundancy is limited and the presentation is more characteristic of the elaboration phase of generalization than of the integrative phase.

When a child traces a square, on the other hand, the information remains constant. The visual impression is that of a square and the tactual-kinesthetic information is that of a square. Such multisensory presentations are redundant in that the *same* information is presented.

One reason why multi-sensory presentations have not been as helpful as was hoped in teaching may be the fact that in practice they are not truly redundant. Sense avenues are used because of their greater efficiency or greater convenience in presenting certain information. At no time, however, is equivalent information presented through more than one sense avenue. The effect of such procedures on the development of generalization is minimal since nothing really new has been added. The child is exposed to one learning situation after another each of which included the same difficulty in integrating with which he started. Integration is only assisted when the information is common while the presentation varies.

The second problem with the concept of redundancy is that of the time factor. To be redundant, the two presentations must occur *at the same point in time.* This temporal simultaneity must be true for the child as well as for the presentation. Thus, the child, who is asked to trace the square, may be expected to have a visual impression of a square while he is obtaining the kinesthetic impression during the tracing performance.

Some children, however, will be found to eliminate one of the presentations. Such a child may trace with his hand but look out the window as he does so. He has reduced the presentation to a uni-sensory one by taking the visual aspects out. He then sees a square at one point in time and experiences a square tactually and kinesthetically at another point in time. Such a time differential further contributes to the lack of integration among his learning experiences rather than helping to organize them. The acute teacher will observe this child's behavior and insure that he watches as he traces thus bringing the two presentations together in time.

This problem of simultaneity may account for the fact that the designers of multi-sensory methods such as Fernald, Gillingham, and others, have traditionally had more success with the method than have others who applied the method. These workers are accomplished clinicians and are aware of differences in the child's performance even though they may not be able to verbalize their nature. In practice, therefore, they spontaneously correct his approach and insure simultaneity in his process. Others using the method are not as aware of atypical approaches by children and are not as skillful in observing their occurrence. Therefore, they do not use the same care to insure that the child is using all the presentations simultaneously. As a result, they are not as successful with the method as was the originator.

Another child may trace a square in a very slow, painstaking manner keeping his eye directly on his hand and being sure that the pencil stays precisely on the line. This child is being redundant about the wrong thing . If the task has been designed to teach pure eye-hand coordination and a precise perceptual-motor match, then his performance is excellent. The visual information and the kinesthetic information are matched and are simultaneous in time. If the task has been designed to teach the perceptual generalization of a square, however, then the performance is faulty. The child had a visual impression of a square before he started. As he began to trace, however, he gave up this impression and now has only an impression of a line. He is merely tracing lines. He is not tracing a square. He is being redundant but the redundancy is not pertinent to the task for which it was designed. The acute teacher would insist that the child give up this painstaking performance and, with less precision and accuracy, trace the outline of the square directing his major attention to the form. Such redundancy of the percept, square, could help to integrate this generalization for the child whereas his former performance would only intensify an element (line) of the form.

A further difficulty with multi-sensory presentations involves the point in the learning process at which they are used. The greatest contribution of these methods comes in the integration of a cluster of similar experiences into a whole. It is evident that such integration cannot take place until such a cluster of learnings has been provided. Therefore, multi-sensory presentations are of minimal value until elaboration has taken place. Frequently teachers begin immediately with multi-sensory presentations under the impression that these are the methods to be used with children who have learning disorders. They are thus attempting to be redundant when the child as yet has nothing to be redundant with. They are attempting to develop integration where there is nothing to integrate. The elaboration resulting from variation in experience should precede multi-sensory presentation. If it does, such presentations may serve to help the child integrate these elaborations. If it does not, the multi-sensory presentation becomes just another datum and, since there is no relation between such data, adds to his confusion. To serve the purposes of redundancy, such presentations must occur in the third stage of the development of generalization and must follow elaboration of the initial datum.

Herein lies another principle in the teaching of generalizations: *When elaboration has been accomplished, the child should be aided in integrating these data through the presentation of the same information in different ways at the same point in time.*

Note that redundancy is the exact opposite of drill. Drill presents the information in the same way at different points in time. Redundancy presents the information in different ways at the same point in time. For the child who is having difficulty generalizing, drill is contraindicated. His response to the initial presentation indicated that he has difficulty learning through this type of presentation. Merely to repeat this presentation can be expected only to increase his difficulty. If he learns from such repeated presentations, it can be expected that his learning will be of the rote memory type and will merely intensify the initial datum thereby impeding rather than fostering generalization.

This is not to say that drill may not be necessary. There are certain facts in education which must be learned by drill procedures and which can be expected to remain rote memory items. The addition and subtraction combinations are an illustration. These addition and subtraction facts, however, do not teach numerical generalizations. Their memorization does not insure ability in mathematical manipulations or meaning in numerical relations.

The oft-quoted recommendation that the slow learner needs drill and more drill can be expected to lead to nothing more than a collection of isolated facts. This child, because of his difficulties in generalization, needs teaching designed to foster the development of concepts on all levels. To load him with more drill only increases his problems. Drill may be important for him but it will become important only after the basic concept has been developed, not before. When he understands the basic generalizations of arithmetic, then the addition and subtraction facts can be supplied him through drill.

LEVELS OF GENERALIZATION

Concept Level. As has been pointed out earlier, the school has been concerned traditionally with the development of generalization on the concept and symbolic levels. Care has been taken to present information in a systematized manner so that organized bodies of subject matter were presented to the child. Experimentation has been extensive in the area of concept formation and conceptual manipulations. The stages in the development of generalization outlined previously were, for the most part, identified through research in conceptual and symbolic learning.

Percept Level. Not so much attention has been paid, however, to development of generalizations on the percept level. Strauss[1] and others have emphasized the importance of organization and integration in perception and have designed teaching techniques based on the development of such integration in the child. Form perception, figure-ground relationships, form constancy, size constancy, and the like may be thought of as generalizations in the area of perception.

It seems logical to suppose that these perceptual generalizations are in every way like the generalizations on the concept level with which we are more familiar. They appear to develop in the same

[1] Strauss, A. A., and Kephart, N. C., *Psychopathology and Education of the Brain Injured Child.* Volume II: *Progress in Theory and Clinic.* New York: Grune and Stratton, 1955, pp. 47-89.

way and to serve the same purpose. They are true generalizations involving clusters of experience organized and integrated so that unique qualities emerge.

It follows that the teaching of perceptual generalization is similar to the teaching of symbolic generalization. The same elaborations of initial data and the same integration among these elaborations are required. In the perceptual area the data are perceptual elements, units of a total perception. Hebb[2] has pointed out that the basic perceptual elements are lines and angles. These units are combined into integrated perceptual wholes with abstracted qualities, just as are the units of information which enter into the concept.

We are more apt to take such perceptual generalizations for granted because they normally occur at an earlier developmental level and the child usually comes to us with such generalizations well established. In a large number of children, however, these basic perceptual generalizations are not well established. They are not able to combine the elements of a perceptual experience into integrated wholes. Such functions as form perception, figure-ground, and the like are, therefore, not firmly established. When these children are thrust into the many activities of the classroom which require efficient manipulation of these functions, they experience difficulty and confusion results. As the manipulations required become more complex, the confusion becomes greater and failure and frustration are apt to result.

Particularly at the elementary grades, education needs to give attention to the status of these perceptual generalizations in the child. Where they are not established, teaching techniques are required as a part of the classroom activities which will aid in their development. Without such perceptual abilities, the child can be expected to experience greater and greater difficulty as his school experience progresses.

---

[2]Hebb, D. O., *The Organization of Behavior,* Springfield, Ill.: C. C. Thomas, 1955.

It is important to note that these perceptual generalizations are more than mere perceptual differentiations. Particularly in beginning reading, much attention is given to perceptual differentiation. In the visual area, the child is taught to differentiate between similar shapes, including, especially, letters and figures. In the auditory area, he is taught to differentiate between similar sounds, especially those used in our language. Such differentiation, however, is concerned primarily with the development of perceptual elements. It is designed to increase the number of such elements which can be identified. Although differentiation is important to the development of generalization, it is only part of the problem. The organization between these differentiated elements is equally important. This latter problem is frequently given little attention in the classroom. For the child with learning disabilities, however, it is frequently the most difficult problem which he faces. It is, therefore, important that the same attention be given to the teaching of these perceptual generalizations as is given to the teaching of symbolic generalizations. The principles of such teaching are essentially the same, only the type of element with which we are dealing is different.

Motor Level. It is even less common to think of motor activities of the child in terms of the principle of generalization. It would appear, however, that these motor responses become integrated and organized into wholes in the same way that perceptual elements or symbolic information does. Basic coordination and motor problem solving are based on such generalizations in the motor area. Thus, walking is a motor skill or pattern. It consists of a series of movements which result in putting one foot in front of the other and moving the body forward. Locomotion, on the other hand, is a motor generalization.[3] It consists of a large

---

[3] Dunsing, J. D., and Kephart, N. C., *Motor Generalizations in Space and Time,* in Hellmuth, J. (ed.), *Learning Disorders,* Volume I. Seattle: Special Child Publications, 1965.

collection of specific movements (walking, running, hopping, crawling, rolling, and the like) which result in moving the body through space. Furthermore, the child can use any or all of these specific movements as the requirements of the situation demand without directing his attention to how the movement is going to be made. He can direct all his attention to the purpose of the movement. Only through such extensive motor generalizations, can the child's complete attention be free for the exploration necessary to organize the environment around him or for a response to that environment.

As was pointed out earlier, the base for organizing the environment and for the development of the perceptual and conceptual generalizations is established through systematic motor exploration. Such systematic exploration requires the uninterrupted attention of the child. Motor generalizations are, therefore, important in permitting uninterrupted and systematic exploration. In like manner, systematic response to the environment requires a motor activity which is sufficiently flexible that it can be controlled with only a monitoring function. Thus, when the child attempts to write, it is necessary that the movements of the hand take place under the monitoring of the eye. If the child must stop and think how each movement is to be made, writing becomes very difficult. Such continuous monitoring permits control of the response on the basis of continuous incoming information. It is possible only when motor generalizations have been established. With only motor skills, attention to the information necessary in the problem solving must be diluted by attention to the nature and process of the movement.

Much attention is given in education to the development of motor skills. Normative data suggest certain acts which a child of a given chronological age should be able to perform. The child is then directly taught to perform this motor act. Too frequently, however, such teaching results in the development of a specific skill in this particular act and for this particular purpose. It has little relationship to any other activities of the child and cannot be used for any other purposes. It represents a sort of parlor trick which the child has learned and can demonstrate upon request but has little usefulness in augmenting his response to his environment.

Ismail and Gruber[4] have demonstrated that overall motor coordination is highly related to academic success among elementary school children. Such a relationship was not found between motor skills and achievement. Such factors as balance, laterality, gross muscle coordination, and the like were the effective variables in relation to learning. Their study further suggests that attention to these generalized motor functions can produce increased achievement in school tasks among elementary school children.

It would, therefore, appear that the school should give attention, through its physical education and similar programs, to the development of motor generalizations. Such generalizations on the motor level serve the same types of purposes in the learning of the child as do the perceptual and conceptual generalizations. They can be taught through the same principles of teaching. Only the elements with which we deal are different.

If education is to be maximally effective in the life of the child, it must result in the development of generalization. Without this function, educational materials become a mere collection of facts. Unless such facts are brought together and organized, they are not readily available to the child for the solution of his problems. Many children have specific difficulty in putting these learning data together into organized wholes so that they can be applied in a variety of situations rather than only in the specific situation in which they were presented. Teaching procedures designed to promote the development of such generalizations are needed, not only for the child with a particular problem but for all children as

[4] Ismail, A. H., and J. J. Gruber, *Integrated Development: Motor Aptitude and Intellectual Performance.* Columbus: Chas. E. Merrill, 1967.

well. Such development is basic to the success of education. These generalizations exist not only on the level of academic information but on the perceptual and motor levels as well. The school should give major attention to such teaching on all levels of development if it is to promote the maximum achievement of each child according to his potential.

Chapter IV

Representative Teaching Activities

THE PURPOSE of this chapter is to suggest some learning situations which can be presented to the child and which can aid him in the learning of those types of activities which are known in education as readiness skills. Learning disorders frequently lead to breakdowns in the course of development. When the learning interference begins at an early age, certain developmental skills will not be achieved or will be learned inadequately. Later developing skills may thereby be disrupted and the classroom learnings of the school may be rendered difficult or impossible.

For these reasons, it has been suggested that the public school will need to give attention to the teaching of readiness skills and activities which are normally assumed to be possible for the child when he enters school. For the most part, it would be expected that such teaching would take place in the classroom and within the pattern of classroom situations. The learning situations described herein are, therefore, those which can be fitted into classroom activities without too much disruption of the group. There are, of course, more intensive training and therapeutic techniques suitable for the clinic or special class setting. Such more intensive techniques may be necessary for certain children and at certain stages in their development. What is described herein is, therefore, a selected group of learning presentations and is not to be considered a complete therapeutic program for any child. In mild cases, these procedures may be sufficient to permit success in school achievement. In more severe cases, more intensive study and help will be necessary.

Neither is the present description meant to be a complete class-room program for dealing with children with learning disorders. By definition, the learning processes and teaching requirements of these children are atypical. It is, therefore, not possible to write a "cookbook" for their education. Each individual child has unique needs and unique problems. The teacher must constantly revise, delete, and augment any program which might be suggested, in terms of the unique requirements of the child. No technique is "good" for all children and, by the same token, no technique is "bad" for all children. Techniques are but suggestions of possible ways to approach certain types of problems. Their actual application must be determined by the teacher on the basis of his understanding of the needs of the children, on the one hand, and the nature of the technique, on the other. Modifications and alterations will *always* be required and should be made without hesitation when the need arises. The following descriptions are, therefore, to be considered only as suggestions to point out the kinds of class-room activities which can be used to help solve the learning problems of such children.

In addition, as has been pointed out earlier, the problem is not to teach individual skills but to teach generalizations. For this purpose, constant variation of any basic activity must be presented to the child. Equally important with the procedure itself is the ability to suggest many variations. Such variations cannot be thoroughly described because they must grow out of and be related to the particular situation of the classroom. If they are not thus related to an immediate situation, they tend to become artificial and lose much of their effectiveness.

Therefore, the activities presented are to be considered as a bare core of teaching procedures and not as a complete method. This bare core must be given life and vitality by the creative efforts of the teacher in introducing related activities and adequate variations. Occasionally, the more obvious variations will be mentioned. These also are to be considered as illustrations not as a complete description of a finished or prescribed set of desirable variations.

Gross Motor Activities

Many children with learning disorders will be found to have very limited motor responses. Such limitations are particularly apparent in the areas of relationship to gravity, laterality, and overall coordination. Since basic information originates in motor exploration and is stabilized through a motor referent, such limitations can be expected to interfere with the child's extent of learning and particularly with his ability to organize information in a veridical fashion.

Normally, these gross motor activities would be centered in the physical education department of the school. It should be pointed out, however, that the interest in physical education in this connection is in the development of general motor responses, motor patterns and motor generalizations, not in the development of physical skills, important as these may be. The physical education program, therefore, for this purpose, must be a very broad one and must include activities concerned with the motor adjustment of the child to the environment around him. It must aim toward the establishment of motor responses as a means of gathering and coordinating information. When such extensions of activities are included, the physical education program becomes more than an auxillary aspect of education. Its contribution is seen as a vital part of the educational process. Physical education is then used, in a very real sense, "to help children learn to read."

In many school systems, however, the physical education program is too limited both quantitatively and qualitatively to serve this more extensive purpose, particularly at the elementary level. Qualitatively, the program lacks the broad expanse of motor experiences necessary to provide a motor basis for learning. Too frequently, the program concentrates overly closely on the development of skills required in sports and games. The child who cannot perform becomes a mere spectator, although he is the one in the entire group most in need of the experience. Little opportunity for motor experimentation or elaboration of new found skills and abilities is provided.

Quantitatively, the program is frequently limited to one or two half-hour periods per week. It is felt that, in the first three grades, a minimum of one hour per day of active participation in gross motor activities is desirable. The child needs much opportunity to explore his new world, and, through his motor activity, to relate it in a meaningful fashion to what has gone before. Such veridical structuring of the new fine motor, perceptual, and symbolic material to which he is being introduced requires much time in motor experimentation and physical contact with relationships in the concrete world about him.

Frequently the physical education program becomes more intensive both quantitatively and qualitatively at the later grade levels. From the point of view stressed here, however, the most urgent needs are at the elementary level. The greatest contribution to overall learning can probably be made in the grade range K through 3. This is often, however, the very grade range which has the least program provided. It is thought that, especially for the child with learning disorders, a marked strengthening both quantitative and qualitative of the physical education program at the early elementary grades will be required if the educational needs of children are to be met adequately.

Where sufficient physical education programs do not exist, the present program will need to be augmented by further gross motor activities presented by the classroom teacher. These additional activities may be under the direction of the physical education department or they may be the responsibility of the classroom teacher. In either event, sufficient time should be provided in the school day to permit an adequate program.

Furthermore, although these activities will be and should remain group oriented, provision should be made in the planned procedures for special aid to the child who shows a specific problem. Such a child should be helped to perform rather than being sidetracked. Lesson plans should be flexible so that a child can concentrate in the area of his need for motor experimentation rather than be subjected to a regimented series of prescribed performances.

Equipment. Although many of the activities in a motor training program require no equipment, it is well to provide simple devices, particularly in the balance and coordination areas, which permit more extensive experimentation. A set composed of a number of units will provide more efficient programs than will single pieces of equipment which are not related to each other in purpose. A number of such sets of simple equipment are available. One such is the Prudden-Porter Gymster.[1]

The Gymster contains equipment for balance and coordination as well as simple stunts and exercises to develop strength of muscle. It is compact and requires little space for its use and hence can be used in a classroom as well as in a gymnasium or all-purpose room. It folds compactly and stores in a small space. It does not require bolting down to floor or wall. It is suitable for both group and individual work and, with proper spotting, is safe. Its cost is modest enough to make it practical for use in small systems or with small groups within a system.

The set consists of two wooden "T"-beams 7-½ feet long. These beams are shaped like a railroad rail, the base being 5 inches wide and the rail being 2 inches wide. These beams fit into brackets on folding tubular steel bases so that they can be raised above the floor. Provided are three bases 12 inches high, one base 21 inches

---

[1] Prudden-Porter Gymster, available from Porter Athletic Equipment, 9555 Irving Park Road, Schiller Park, Ill.

FIGURE 4
The Prudden-Porter Gymster.

high and one 30 inches high. There is also a wooden ladder 6 feet 8 inches long which can be fitted into the notches of the steel stands. There is a wooden rocker, 5 feet long, with a curved bottom so that the child can stand on it and rock back and forth. An attachment to the stands allows the teacher to convert one of the "T"-beams into a teeter-totter. A plastic hoop and wand to provide objects to jump over or through complete the set.

One advantage of an integrated set of equipment is that the pieces can be used separately or can be connected together to provide more complex tasks. Such equipment should be flexible so that many kinds of activity can be designed with each piece of the material. As will be seen below a basic piece of equipment can be used for many kinds of experience if it is sufficiently flexible. Because of the need for experimentation and the requirement for variation in activity, a few pieces of basic equipment which are flexible are more desirable than more extensive equipment which is designed for a specific purpose. It is for this reason that basic sets of equipment can provide, with a limited financial outlay, a great wealth of experience for the child.

The following account illustrates some of the uses of the Prudden-Porter Gymster in classroom situations.

Balance. Lay the "T"-beam along a mat with the 2-inch surface up. The child walks the length of the beam balancing so as not to step off as he does so. He walks forward across the board,

FIGURE 5
An obstacle as a variation in a balancing task.

then repeats the task walking backward across the board. He then faces at right angles to the board and walks across sidewise in a right to left direction. The latter task is repeated, the child walking in a left to right direction.

The teacher should help the child who has major balance problems by holding on to his hand. However, he should be encouraged to dispense with this help as soon as he is able. If the child cannot manage the beam at all, the two beams can be placed parallel to each other on the mat with a short distance separating them. The beams thus form an "alley" within which the child is asked to walk. As he gains balancing proficiency, the two beams are moved closer together thus providing a narrower "alley." This procedure is continued until the child can manage the single beam in the customary manner.

Variations can be introduced into the balancing task by requiring various maneuvers during the child's progress across the board. He can be asked to walk half way across, stop and balance while standing still, then proceed. He can be asked to walk half way, turn and come back.

Further variations can be introduced by presenting an obstacle to the child. Hold the wand across the beam at right angles and resting on the upper surface. Ask the child to step over the wand as he walks down the beam. Increase the difficulty by gradually raising the height of the wand above the surface. Hold the hoop level to the ground and resting on the beam. Ask the child to walk over the hoop. Gradually raise the height of the hoop above the beam. Hold the wand at shoulder height and ask the child to duck under it. Hold the hoop vertically, facing the child, and ask him to walk through it.

The difficulty of the balance task can also be increased by raising the beam above the mat. This can be accomplished by placing one of the 12-inch bases under each end of the beam. (It is desirable to provide a "spotter" when the beam is raised.) Raising the beam increases the difficulty primarily through its effect on the visual aspects of balance and the increased demand for a visual orientation to space, which parallels the motor orientation to gravity.

At first the task should be simplified by turning the beam upside down. In this position a rail 5 inches wide on which to balance is provided for the child. When his ability increases, the beam can be turned over so that he must balance on a 2-inch surface.

Variations can be introduced in the raised beam task by placing the beam on a slant. Place one end of the beam on the floor and the other end on the 12-inch base, or place a 12-inch base under one end and a 21-inch base under the other. When the slanted beam is used, the direction of the line of gravity through the body must be used as the clue for balance not the position of the body with reference to the surface. When the beam is flat, both gravity and body position are perpendicular to the surface. When the board is slanted, these two clues are different. The slanted board, therefore, serves to emphasize the line of gravity as the basis for balance by separating this factor from orientation to the surface. For this reason some children will find this slanted surface much more difficult to deal with.

Further variation can be introduced by using the two beams in combination. The beams are laid end to end but at right angles so that the child walks down one, turns a right angle, and walks down the other. One rail can be raised and the other not so that the child walks down one, steps down (or up), and walks down the other. Different slants of the two rails can be provided. Many combinations, along with the variations suggested for a single rail, can be worked out so that a constant variation in balancing performance is demanded.

Further balance problems can be provided by altering the position in which the child performs. In addition to the standing position, three positions will be found useful: (1) Duck walk— the knees are bent and the child walks in a squat position. (2) Cat walk—the child walks in an "all-fours" position. Vary by requiring that the knees be kept straight (monkey walk). (3) Crab walk—the child squats down with hands behind him on the board but without sitting down. The child should walk both forward and backward in each of the three positions in combination with as many of the suggested variations as possible.

A different approach to balance involves balancing on the arms. The beam is raised to the 21-inch height. The child sits straddle-legged on the beam. He places his hands on the beam in front of him, leans forward lifting his seat off the beam and balances on his arms. The child may move across the beam by lifting onto his arms, swinging his seat forward to his hands and repeating until he

FIGURE 6
Adjusting balance to the activities of another.

has crossed the board. Some children may be able to "walk" across the board on their hands by alternating hands, keeping the seat off the beam.

A very important variation of the balance problem involves the cooperation of two children. Place the two beams on the mat parallel to each other and about 20 inches apart. Two children hold hands and one walks down each beam. Not only must each child adjust his balancing activities to those of the other as well as to gravity but he must pace his movements in rhythm with those of the other. The problem can be varied by varying the distance between the beams. A form of continuous variation results if the beams are placed in the form of a "V."

Laterality.[2] It is important that the child distinguish motor activities on the right side of his body from those on the left side. It is also important that he learn to shift easily and smoothly from one side to another. Activities which contrast action on one side with that on the other contribute to such learning.

Laterality is concerned in most of the balancing tasks described previously. When balance is lost, compensatory movements and shifts must frequently be made either on one side alone or disproportionately on the two sides. Thus, if flexibility is stressed in the maintenance of balance, a large number of the balancing activities can be used to teach laterality as well.

It should be stressed that such learning takes place only when the child is engaged in restoring balance. When the child performs the task without losing balance, little or no learning takes place. Care should, therefore, be taken to see that the child is presented tasks carefully selected so that he deals with a balance *problem* and with compensatory movements necessary to establish or regain balance. Thus, both tasks which are too easy, so that balance is never lost, and those which are too hard, so that balance is never

---

[2] For a discussion of laterality, see Kephart, N. C., *The Slow Learner in the Classroom.* Columbus: Chas. E. Merrill, 1960.

FIGURE 7

The crab walk on two beams.

established, should be avoided since neither task contributes to learning.

The nature of activities on the two sides can be emphasized by using two beams. The beams are placed parallel and side by side. The child places his right foot on one beam and his left foot on the other. He then moves down the track keeping each foot on its own beam. This activity requires a shift of both weight and movement from one side to the other alternately. The shift is made more intense than it is in ordinary walking by the prescribed position of the feet and the balance problem introduced by the beams. These effects can be further exaggerated by moving the beams further apart.

Lateral movement can also be emphasized by the use of the

FIGURE 8
Teaching laterality with a rocking device.

rocker board. Lay the device on the mat and ask the child to stand on it facing one side and with his feet wide apart. As he shifts his weight from one side to the other, the device rocks back and forth. Variations can be introduced by changing the distance between the feet. Such activity is especially useful to teach a smooth flow of movement from one side of the body to the other.

Adaptation to lateral movement is illustrated if three children use the rocker simultaneously. In this case, two children stand, one at each end and facing each other. The third stands in the middle

FIGURE 9

*Crossed arms and legs emphasize laterality
and body image.*

with his feet apart facing sidewise. The two children on the ends then spring lightly up and down alternately, causing the device to rock back and forth. The child in the center must adjust to this lateral change and maintain his balance.

These examples illustrate lateral responses primarily of the legs and lower trunk. Similar responses of the arms and shoulders can be illustrated by the game of wheelbarrow. In this game, one child grasps the legs of a second and holds them off the floor while the second child moves forward on his hands. Since the problem of interest is laterality, it is well for the child to grasp the "wheelbarrow" high on the thighs rather than at the calves or ankles. Thus, the movement of the arms and shoulders is stressed rather than the strength of legs or back. The child should be encouraged to move his arms and shoulders and not to roll back and forth at the hips.

The game can be played on the mat alone, on the parallel beams, on a single beam or on the ladder laid along the floor. The movement required can be in a forward direction, a backward direction, or a sidewise direction.

Lateral movements of both arms and legs simultaneously can be illustrated on the parallel beams. In this case, the child stands with both feet on one beam facing sidewise. He then bends forward and places his hands on the other beam. In this position, he walks sidewise down the track.

The difference between the two sides can be accentuated by asking the child to cross one foot or arm over the other. In this position, he is asked to "walk" to his left by moving his right foot behind his left, shifting his weight onto it and bringing his left foot around in front of it. On the next trial, he may be asked to cross the right foot ahead of the left. Such crosses can be prescribed with the child moving in either direction.

He can be asked to "walk" crossing his arms in the same manner. These arm crossings can then be made to either parallel or reverse the crossings of the legs. The same type of activities can be performed with the child in the "crab" position rather than the "all-fours" position.

It may be found that these activities in which limbs are crossed involve body image problems as well as laterality problems. The child may have difficulty estimating the space required for his limb to pass. He may find that he loses control of the limb and cannot determine in which direction it should move when it is in the unaccustomed position. He may even lose awareness of a limb during the task. Thus, this activity can also be used to increase body image, awareness, and differentiation particularly in the arms and legs.

Locomotion. Locomotion involves moving the body through space. In many children, such activities will be found to be limited almost entirely to the more common skills of locomotion, walking or running. They may show little ability to traverse space by any means other than walking or running. Furthermore, their skills of walking may be very inflexible so that a minor alteration of the conditions of walking causes them trouble. A simple obstacle or interference may require them to stop and think about the problem of moving. Attention is thus diverted from the goal of the locomotion to the nature of the locomotion.

Such children will need a broader experience in the processes of locomotion. They will need to experiment with locomotion under various types of conditions. Such variations may be provided by altering the surface upon which the locomotion takes place. Walking on a yielding surface such as deep sand, the canvas of a soft mat, irregular ground, etc., represent examples of such variation in the nature of the surface. The child will need to locomote among a number of obstacles where rather frequent changes of direction (right, left, up, down) are required and where he is required to pursue a goal while skirting these obstacles. He will need experience with other types of locomotion than walking or running, such as jumping, hopping, rolling, etc. In all these activities he will need to be presented with a goal so that he is encouraged to develop flexibility of movement in order that he can maintain his attention on the goal.

The process of walking can be altered by laying the ladder down along the floor. The child is first asked to walk down the length of the ladder stepping alternately in each hole between the rungs. He is then asked to walk stepping on each rung.

Such activities prescribe the length of stride and thus alter his normal walking skill. Longer strides can be prescribed by asking him to step in every other hole or on every other rung. Irregular strides can be prescribed by asking him to step in one, skip a hole, step in the next, etc.

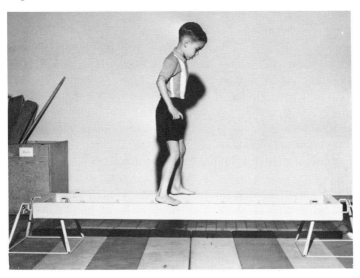

FIGURE 10
Varying the walking stance.

A variation in the walking stance can be produced by asking the child to place one foot on each side of the frame of the ladder and walk to the end. This activity is much like walking down the parallel beams except that here the emphasis is on the goal at the end of the ladder rather than the balancing or laterality task at each stage.

An irregular step can be introduced by asking the child to step alternately on the rungs and in the holes. In this activity he lifts his weight higher on one step than he does on the next.

FIGURE 11
Varying the walking stride.

The difficulty of these activities can be increased and the alteration of the walking task can be emphasized if the ladder is raised above the floor by placing the ends on the 12-inch stands. Walking in the holes of the ladder now requires an abnormally high step. Walking alternately on rungs and holes requires a marked rise of the body on alternate steps.

An inclined surface for locomotion can be provided by inverting the "T" beam and placing one end on a stand and the

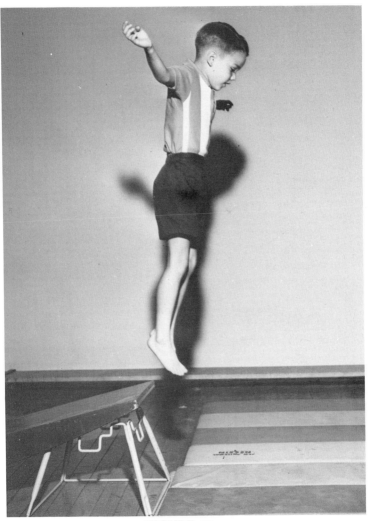

FIGURE 12
Jumping as locomotion.

other on the floor. The child can now walk up or down an inclined plank. He should perform these tasks in both the forward and backward direction. A similar incline can be provided by propping one end of the rocker board on a stand with the other end on the floor. In addition to walking on an incline, the child can now also roll on an incline since the board is wide enough to permit such tasks. He can roll down (or up) the hill both laterally or by a front or back roll. Again, the attention is called to the goal of "getting down (or up) the hill" rather than to the movement itself. Rolling is presented as a form of locomotion. On a flat surface, crossing a mat by rolling presents the same type of task. The child should roll forward and backward. In a lateral roll, he should move to his right and also to his left.

Jumping is another form of locomotion. This activity includes a jump in which one leg leads (a modification of walking) and a jump in which the two legs leave the ground together (two-legged jump). Hopping is a one-footed jump which adds a balance problem to the task.

The child can be asked to move down the ladder which is laid along the floor by jumping from one hole to the next. A one-legged or a two-legged jump can be prescribed. He can be asked to cross a mat by jumping or he can be asked to jump over a wand held close to the floor.

Jumping from a height presents locomotion in a vertical direction as well as accenting the force of gravity. The "T"-beam or rocker board can be placed in the inclined position. The child is asked to walk up the board and jump off the end. Attention is placed on the goal so that these two locomotor activities are integrated rather than being kept separate and distinct. If the wand is held in front of the board, the child can be encouraged to jump far ahead. If it is held higher than the end of the board, he can be encouraged to jump high and far. Jumps with one foot or with both feet together can be called for.

Jumping activities may be combined with orientation tasks in which directional changes in space are combined with the jumping movements. Thus, the child is asked to jump up and turn a quarter or half turn while in the air. He is first asked to describe how he will be facing and what will be in front of him if he successfully completes the task. The preliminary orientation stresses for him the spacial relations of the task and the orientation problem involved. He then performs a movement which will produce the predicted orientation.

Such orientation problems can also be combined with the task of jumping from a height. The rocker board is placed with one end elevated on a stand. First the child is asked to jump off the board backwards. This task presents to many children a major alteration of orientation as well as a major alteration of locomotion. The turning in air described previously can then be presented, starting either from a forward position or a backward position. Various combinations of direction in both walking up the board and jumping off the end can be combined with various turns to create complex problems of locomotion and orientation in a single task.

A further alteration of locomotor activities is provided by changes in pace. Many children will be found who have trouble changing the pace of simple motor activities. Thus, they can walk in a given pace but lose the pattern if asked to change the speed. They are unable to alter the pace without disrupting the basic locomotor skill and producing confusion. Most of the activities described can be paced. Such pacing can be achieved by introducing music into the activity and asking the child to perform in time to the music. If the maintenance of such rhythm to music is too difficult for the child, pacing can be achieved through a simple drum beat or by clapping the hands to rhythm. The child is then asked to pace each step to the beat of the rhythm.

Coordination. Laterality is dependent upon the differentiation between the two sides of the body. In addition to such differentiation, it is necessary that the child be able to coordinate the movements of the two sides. The sides must work together in the accomplishment of a task and the child must be aware of the difference at all times. Sometimes movements on the two sides are

FIGURE 13
Coordinating the four quadrants of the body.

parallel; sometimes they are reversed. There must be an ability to shift flexibly from one form of movement to the other without losing awareness of the side and what it is doing.

In addition to the relationship between the two sides, there must also be a relationship between the top half of the body and the bottom half. Patterns of movement occur between the two vertical halves as they do between the two lateral halves. These movements must be coordinated and the child must be aware of what is happening.

There are, thus, four quadrants which need to be coordinated. This coordination should include all types of movement and all types of relationships between the movement of the quadrants. Swimming is an example of cross lateral coordination in which complex movements of arms and legs are integrated into a total pattern of movement which accomplishes a purpose. The child should be able to integrate such complexes and maintain them without undue attention to the movements themselves. The difference between the swimming pattern and that of the bear walk, the rabbit hop, and other stunts will illustrate the combinations of the four quadrants needed for various types of movement.

It is through these coordinated activities that most of the exploratory movements of the child will be made. It is, therefore, necessary that these patterns be well established so that the child can be free to evaluate the results of the movement. In addition to its importance in free exploration, many of the tasks which we set for the child involve such coordinated movements. Even where overt movements are not required, a similar coordinated pattern is needed to maintain balance and orientation to the task. The Ismail and Gruber study found measures of such coordination to correlate highly with school achievement in elementary school children. Their study emphasizes the importance of coordination in the learning activities of the child.

More complex activities with simple equipment can serve to

illustrate coordination and to help the child in his development. When the ladder is placed on the two 12-inch bases, a bridge is formed. The child can be asked to step or climb over the bridge or to crawl under it. When he crawls under the ladder it is low enough that he must pull himself along on his stomach to get through. If a higher base is used he can crawl through on his hands and knees. Both of these tasks represent patterns of coordination between the four quadrants.

When the ladder is on the 12-inch bases, the child may be

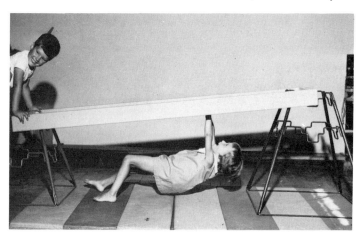

FIGURE 14
*Coordinating the upper half and the lower half
of the body.*

asked to stand on the rims, lean forward and place his hands on the rungs. He can then walk across the ladder. A variation is provided if he is asked to put his feet on the rungs instead of the rims. These tasks can be performed backwards as well as forwards. A further variation is the "monkey walk" is which the child crosses the ladder as before but with the legs held stiff and straight. It is desirable, in these activities, that the parts work together. The child should be discouraged from moving his arms first and then later moving his legs to catch up.

Set one end of the ladder on one of the bases so that a ramp is formed. All the activities previously described can now be performed again but in this activity the angle of the surface is changed, introducing more difficulty and more complications. For many children this change of angle will prove quite difficult, particularly when going down the ladder since the weight is thrown forward in a manner to which they are not accustomed. If the "crab walk" is performed on this tilted ladder, the problems can be made quite difficult.

Place the ladder at the 21-inch height. For young children, this permits hanging by the arms with the seat off the ground but the feet touching. In this position, ask the child to perform a pull-up raising his chin up to the ladder by pulling with his arms. If the child is at an angle to the ladder, the feet will be dragged along the floor as he pulls up. Such activity presents another type of relation between the body parts. The feet and legs must be alternately cut out of the activity and then brought back in. It is sometimes as difficult for a child to cut out a part or parts as it is to include it in an activity. This task, therefore, presents another kind of coordination problem.

Forward and backward rolls require coordination of the four quadrants. These rolls can be performed on the mat or they can be performed from a height. Place one end of the "T"-beam or the rocker board on the 12-inch base. The child then walks or climbs up the ramp and performs a forward roll off the end by bending over the end, placing his shoulders in position on the mat, then lifting his legs over. The same activity can be performed backwards, ending in a backward roll.

Experimentation. The development of motor patterns or motor generalizations requires extensive experimentation. The ele-

FIGURE 15
*Motor problem solving: Go down through one hole and
up through the next.*

ments of such combinations can be taught specifically. Their
integration into a generalization, however, is largely the result of
the child's experimentation. It is through such experimentation that
he works out the relationships between movements and combines
them into useful wholes. Therefore, in any program of gross motor
activity, much time should be provided for experimentation.

In addition to such free experimentation, it is well to foster or
encourage experimentation by setting the task so that motor
problem solving is required. Such problem solving is demanded when
the task is left unstructured for the child. In general, there are
four levels of structuring which the teacher can present to the
child. The first of these is a simple statement of the task. In the
balance beam, for example, this level is illustrated by the command,
"Walk to the end of the board." The child is given only the goal
of the activity and must work out for himself how this goal is to
be reached.

The second level involves a verbal description of the movements involved. Thus, the teacher might say, "Step up on the board, now put this foot ahead, now step up to that foot, etc." The task is broken down into single movements, thus reducing the complexity of the problem. However, the child is required to work out each movement for himself.

The third level is the level of demonstration. The teacher walks down the board and asks the child to imitate his performance. At this stage the child has the movements fully described to him, he sees them performed. He has only to imitate them.

The final level of structuring is concrete. The child's limbs are physically manipulated until they make the correct movements or assume the correct position. This stage represents almost complete structuring. The child need only to repeat movements which have, in effect, been made for him.

The degree of problem solving required of the child decreases rapidly as more and more structuring is introduced. From the point of view of overall learning, the child gains most when he solves his own motor problem. Therefore, it is desirable to start with the first level of structuring and move down the scale only if it appears that the child cannot solve the problem. It is well to permit the child to make a number of mistakes while attempting to solve the problem. It is through these mistakes and the modifications developed to overcome them that he learns most.

In so far as possible, all the activities described should be presented as problem-solving tasks. Interest should always center in the learning that is taking place, not in the quality of the final performance. In addition, it will be found desirable to introduce some tasks which are primarily used for their problem-solving value.

One such task is the game of variations. The child is set the simple task of getting to the other side of a tumbling mat. When he has accomplished this, he is asked to come back another way, to use another method of getting over the mat. This request is repeated, each time demanding another method of locomotion which will accomplish the goal of getting to the other side of the mat. If the child is motivated toward this game, he will make extensive experimentations in the solution of problems of locomotion.

The game can be expanded and the motivation of the children can be extended if the game is changed to "follow the leader." Now the first child in line solves the problem and each other child imitates his solution. On the next turn, the next child becomes the leader, etc. In this activity each child solves the problem by his most common method. Each other child, however, is required to imitate his solution. Since each child has a different favorite method, the follower is required to practice solutions at which he is not adept because they have been prescribed by a child who is more adept. Through this entire series of activities, experimentation and problem solving are "the objects of the game."

For problems involving vertical space, an obstacle high enough to provide a barrier may be presented. For example, the "T"-beam may be placed on the 21-inch bases. At this height, it becomes similar to a vaulting horse. The child is set the problem of getting over the beam. He is then encouraged to develop as many methods of getting over the obstacle as he can.

The beam can be placed on the 12-inch bases. Now the problem is how to get under the beam. The children are encouraged to develop as many ways of solving this problem as they can. Obstacle courses can be set up which involve many objects to walk along, get under, get over, get around, etc. The child is encouraged to solve the problems and then develop his own variations of these solutions.

Fine Motor Coordination

Typical classroom tasks involve coordination of the fine muscula-

ture of the body more intensely than they do the gross muscula-
ture. For the most part, however, these tasks represent extensions
of the learnings resulting from gross activity into more symbolic
or representational phases. Thus, the principle of a right-hand
corner is first learned in gross locomotion around such a corner.
Later it is transferred into the finer movements of the hand and
used to form a part of a square figure. The same spatial relationships involved in the former activity are also involved in the latter.
Although the movements are more confined, they have the same
relationships to outside reality.

A second requirement of most classroom tasks has to do with
the control of the response. In such tasks the control is much more
often perceptual than in more gross activities. Furthermore, the
perceptual data which must be used for control are often representational or symbolic. Pictured materials or print are presented to the
child and he is required to use these perceptual data to monitor his
motor responses. Thus, coloring, tracing, and similar elementary
level activities require that the motor response be confined largely
to the fine muscle systems and that it be guided closely by
perceptual information.

Since emphasis has been laid throughout the gross motor
activities described previously on the purpose of the movement and
on the perceptual information accompanying the activity, a
groundwork has already been laid for the transition of these skills
to the more minute tasks of the classroom. It is essential that
such a transition be made by the child. If it is not, there is
danger that he will learn the manipulations of the classroom
independently. The result will be a body of activity which has
little relationship to the remaining responses of the organism. On
the one hand, two response systems will exist independently with
resulting confusion. On the other hand, the more symbolic activities will lack intensive meaning since they are to a certain
extent independent of, and in some cases conflicting with, the more

FIGURE 16

Gross motor exploration of geometric forms.

concrete experiences of the child.

A transition from concrete reality to representational reality can be provided by activities where the child manipulates materials in a gross manner and then deals with these same materials in a more perceptual or pictorial manner. In one classroom, large forms were laid out on the floor with masking tape (circle, square, triangle, rectangle, diamond). The child was asked to walk around the form and explore it, then to identify it from among a series of forms drawn on the chalkboard. Later he was asked to walk around the form and then draw one like it on the chalkboard. Thus, the gap between gross exploration and the fine exploration of paper and pencil work was bridged for the child.

Similar activities using gross manipulatory skills rather than locomotor skills can be provided by permitting the child to trace around a concrete form to obtain a representation of it. A comparison of concrete objects which can be handled and their pictorial representations may serve a similar purpose. The cut out letters of the alphabet and number symbols used in many kindergarten programs also help to bridge between manipulatory information and the perceptual information which will be used in reading and similar tasks.

When the child begins to produce representational figures for himself, it is desirable that he observe the perceptual data which are produced while he responds. Later he will be asked to control his response by these perceptual data as he is producing them. Thus, in writing or drawing the child uses the perceptual information generated by the act to control the course of the act. In initial stages of learning, however, the child needs to recognize that his movements can, under certain conditions, produce perceptual information; leave a trace, as it were, of the movement. He needs to appreciate the relationship between this trace and the movement which produced it.

At this stage, it is desirable that this perceptual-motor concept be presented in both gross and fine motor responses. In this way, the motor system of the child remains intact and the concept is attached to the entire motoric repertory. Frequently, the relationship involved is inadequately presented in the gross motor area. Paper and pencil tasks are very fine and very precise. Unless similar types of activity more extended in space are provided, the child frequently makes a connection between the task and movements of the fingers and hand but not with the rest of the movement system. The result is one set of specific activities splintered off from the total response of the whole child.

It is, therefore, desirable to provide reproduction activities in a form larger than that of paper and pencil. One useful device for this purpose is the chalkboard. The child should be encouraged to produce marks on the board and to observe the relationship between these marks and the movements which he used to produce

FIGURE 17

Perceptual monitoring on the chalkboard.

them. This is probably one of the major values of scribbling in young children. The child uses scribbling activities to compare the movements which he has learned with their representations. The chalkboard permits such experimentation not only with the fingers and hand but with much larger groups of muscles and much larger types of movement. In addition, the directional relationships of the chalkboard are those of the concrete environment.

"Up" is up and "down" is down. On paper "up" is a conventional direction, "away from you." The chalkboard permits these directional relationships to remain true while the child experiments with the representational aspects of the problem.

Variation in this exploratory activity can be introduced by changing the medium in which the representation is made. Thus, sheets of newsprint can be tacked up on the chalkboard or attached to an easel. With these sheets, paint or crayon can be used. These new media offer a change in the tactual and kinesthetic as well as the visual information generated during the task.

When the directional problem has been worked through, the paper can be laid flat on a desk or table. In this position finger paints are useful. Large sheets of newsprint should be used and the child should stand upright so that more extensive movements are possible. Finger paint is particularly useful because it permits simultaneous experimentation with both sides of the body. Both hands can be used in the paint and the effect upon perceptual information of movements on either side can be compared. In such experimental activities, it is desirable that the child use each side of the body and also both sides simultaneously, so that what he has learned about laterality can be translated through directionality into such reproductive tasks.

When the child understands the relationship between his own movement and the resulting reproductions, he can be urged to guide his performance by outside perceptual data. At this stage, drawing and copying activities can be introduced.[3]

Coloring, tracing, and similar activities of the early elementary grades can also be used. In such activities, the child is taught to use the perceptual information presented or generated during his performance to guide his work. When such learning has been completed, visual monitoring of motor response is possible.

---

[3] For a series of steps in teaching drawing and copying, see *The Slow Learner in the Classroom*, pp. 183-215.

FIGURE 18

Experimenting with the perceptual-motor match
in finger paint.

Most paper and pencil tasks are two dimensional and do not offer possibilities of manipulation during the task. To aid the child in bridging from the three-dimensional world of concrete objects to the two-dimensional world of pictured objects, activities in which three-dimensional representations are produced are useful. Modeling with clay, papier-mâché and the like permit the child to form a three-dimensional reproduction. This reproduction can then be compared with its pictorial representation.

Paper cutting provides an activity in which the product is two dimensional but the process involves manipulation of the material. Such tasks often aid the child in transferring from three to two dimensional representation and in understanding the true nature of the two-dimensional product. The figure-ground relationships in pictured material are frequently emphasized in cutting and pasting tasks where the figure is manipulated independently of the ground.

Where more complex perceptual problems exist, specialized

FIGURE 19
Three-dimensional representations in clay.

procedures to aid in teaching perceptual relationships may be needed. For such cases the materials developed by Frostig will be found useful.[4] These materials are largely paper and pencil exercises designed to present learning situations related to such factors as visual-motor coordination, figure-ground perception, perceptual constancy, position in space, and spatial relationships.

By such activities as these, the child can be aided in transferring his concrete experiences of the environment to pictorial and symbolic representations of such experiences. Through such a process these symbolic materials come to have meaning and to be related to the more concrete experiences. Such meaningfulness permits the child to shift back and forth from symbolic to concrete, from information to response, without confusion and with no interruption of the problem-solving function. The information and activities of school classrooms assume such a close relationship. Without it, many classroom presentations have little meaning for the child and hence little educational value for him.

-----

[4] Frostig, M., and Horne, D., *The Frostig Program for the Development of Visual Perception.* Chicago: Follett Publishing Co., 1964.

Chapter V

Providing Within the System

A s HAS BEEN POINTED OUT, the child with learning disorders has specific problems which affect learning. Because of these problems, many of the customary presentations of the classroom may become meaningless to him. His is quite specifically an educational problem. Whereas other types of handicap interfere with educational procedures in certain ways, this child requires a different type of educational approach.

Special facilities have been provided in the public schools for children with handicaps. For the most part, these children have been segregated into groups determined by categories describing the most obvious handicapping condition. In general, these categories have been mutually exclusive. That is to say, the child is grouped according to his most obvious handicap. If he possesses two or more handicaps, a choice must be made and the child assigned to one class on the basis of this choice. Once having been assigned to this unitary classification, he is given the assistance appropriate to that particular handicap but receives little or no assistance with other handicaps which he may possess. Furthermore, these classifications are usually considered permanent. Thus, when a child has been classified, he remains in this category regardless of changes in his condition or changes in his academic performance.

The customary categories of special education are, for the most part, based on diagnostic findings of professions other than education. Thus, the handicapping conditions identified by this means may be related to education but are not a part of education. An illustration is the category of physically handicapped. These children possess physical characteristics which make certain activities of the public school undesirable or impossible for them. Their learning behavior, however, is not changed. They learn in the same way and through the same procedures as do other children. They require modifications of classroom procedures but not alterations of classroom presentations. The learning content and the learning presentations are as appropriate for these children as for any others. Their problems are medical not educational and the school's responsibility with reference to them is to preserve their medical welfare. From the point of view of the educational process, namely learning, they do not differ from non-handicapped children.

A second classification for which facilities are provided is mentally retarded. The purely mentally retarded (who is not neurologically impaired and thus does not exemplify a learning disorder) learns in essentially the same way as does any other child. His problem is that he learns more slowly and does not learn as complicated material. Here again, normal classroom procedures are essentially adequate. They need only to be modified in terms of scope and sequence to meet the needs of this child.

The blind and the deaf represent classifications of children in whom certain sensory avenues are not available for the transmission of information. Again, learning processes are not materially affected. Only certain areas of presentation must be avoided. These children require a modification of the curriculum which will omit presentations in the sensory areas which are disturbed and present this same material through one of the intact sensory areas. Basically, the presentations of the classroom are adequate, only certain ones have to be omitted. In addition, certain specialized techniques, such as Braille or lip reading, must be introduced into the curriculum. These special techniques, however, can be taught through ordinary teaching techniques and are learned in essentially the same fashion as other learnings, although the mechanics of the process may be somewhat different.

Emotionally disturbed children fall into a category pertinent to psychiatry and psychology. The primary symptoms of this category are behavorial. The concern is with aberrant adjustments to the environment or parts of the environment. When certain pressures occur or certain types of situation arise, the child's behavior becomes bizarre and highly atypical. The learning process, however, is not usually disturbed. Educationally, these children require emotional support but profit from customary teaching methods and techniques. The school's responsibility is to provide support for the emotional instability of the child and undergird thereby the work of other professions. The school is not expected to, nor can it, provide psychotherapy or similar assistance as a part of the educational effort. Where these services are made available, they are added to the functions of the school as a public service and are not considered a part of the teaching task.

The current special education categories, therefore, involve conditions in which modifications of the teaching function are required to take into account certain problems of the child. Such modifications are extremely important and the provision of such special education classes is essential. These problems are not basically failures of the learning process, however, and hence relatively peripheral modifications of purely educational procedures are adequate.

The child with learning disorders, however, represents a handicap directly related to education. In his case, learning processes themselves are disturbed. Ordinary classroom presentations of materials do not suffice. His is a basically educational diagnosis and an educational handicap. For this child, a mere modification of teaching methods and techniques will not suffice. He requires an alteration of learning presentations.

For this reason, these children do not lend themselves to the same type of categorization representative of the classifications of special education as it functions today. Their problems strike at the heart of all education and present a challenge to all teaching. As can be seen from the foregoing discussion, the overt manifestations of their problems are myriad. The specific factors which interfere with the learning of a particular task are multitude. The differences between what is presented and what is perceived cover a large gamut of specifics. For this reason, mere segregation does not insure homogeneous groups for teaching purposes. If such homogeneity could be achieved, a segregated, specialized facility could provide for their needs (as in the case of the mentally retarded). Since such homogeneity is not possible and since their difficulties cover the entire range of educational functions, the customary pattern of specialized facilities seems too narrow and too restricted to accommodate the many needs and many combinations of needs represented in the group of learning disorders.

In addition to being a truly educational classification, learning disorder is associated with higher than normal frequencies of other handicapping conditions. The same factors which gave rise to the learning disorder frequently give rise to other problems as well. Thus, if the interference with learning is sufficiently widespread and sufficiently intense, the child will be mentally retarded as well as a learning disorder. Educationally, he now needs a curriculum reduced in scope and sequence, but he also needs this reduced curriculum presented in an altered fashion. He requires educational procedures appropriate for mentally retarded and, at the same time, he needs educational procedures appropriate for the child with learning disorders. If the neurological disorder strikes the proper area, the child is apt to display physical handicaps in addition to his learning problem. In like manner, sensory impairment may be related to his overall condition.

Learning disorder cuts across the currently established categories. To establish a new category which will encompass those children with learning disorders but no other handicapping condition, is to artificially restrict children and the school's contribution to their educational needs. It means cutting the child to fit the category. Rather, it seems desirable to consider the needs of these children on the basis of their learning behavior and to provide for these needs wherever and whenever they occur throughout their school experience. Since theirs is an educational handicap it seems more appropriate to handle it as a problem of total education, not as some educational sideline which may detract from rather than enhance the regular business of education. When learning disorder is seen in this broader setting, it may provide the basis for better education for all children as well as that group which is its immediate concern.

Facilities

From this point of view, it would appear that three types of facility should be provided to cover adequately the range and complexity of the problems of these children.

Classroom Management. A large number of such children have interferences with learning which are relatively limited. Although the difficulty which they display is probably in itself maximal, it extends over a very limited area of learning. It would appear that, when an interference exists, its effect is largely "all-or-none." Thus, the television writer described earlier suffered from double vision. This condition interfered maximally with certain of his activities. There was not a question of a little double vision being less hampering than a lot of double vision. When double vision exists, it interferes with certain learnings by virtue of its existence.

Such interference, however, may be limited to a relatively small number of classroom activities. Thus, the television writer did not experience such interference in verbal or auditory presentations. Further, he had at his command a large number of other skills and abilities which he could use to compensate for his visual disabilities. Thus, from the point of view of the overall problem of learning, his problems were limited as his achievement in the face of this problem attests.

Children whose difficulties are thus limited have more to gain from association with their peers in the classroom and more to gain from the bulk of classroom presentations than they do from intensive treatment of their problems in isolation. It is, therefore, felt that such children should be dealt with in the regular classroom situation and should not be segregated from their peers.

To handle such problems in the classroom, however, suggests the need for information on the part of the classroom teacher. This teacher should know enough about such problems to be able to observe them in classroom situations and be able to investigate such observed behaviors from the point of view of the effects of possible learning disorders. He needs to know enough to make a screening diagnosis for purposes of referral or of suggested alterations in classroom procedure for this child.

Such simple, teacher-oriented diagnostic instruments are available. In the motor and perceptual-motor area, the Purdue Perceptual-Motor Survey[1] has been standardized. In the perceptual area, the Frostig Developmental Test of Visual Perception[2] has been designed for teacher use. In the more advanced perceptual and conceptual levels, the Illinois Test of Psycholinguistic Abilities[3] offers diagnostic evaluation. This latter instrument is somewhat more difficult for teachers to administer directly but results in findings which are easily interpretable in classroom terms.

In addition to information concerned with identification, the classroom teacher should have information concerning the more

---

[1] Roach, E. G., and N. C., Kephart, *The Purdue Perceptual-Motor Survey*. Columbus: Chas. E. Merrill, 1966.

[2] Frostig, M., *Marianne Frostig Developmental Test of Visual Perception*. Palo Alto, Calif.: Consulting Psychologists Press, 1961.

[3] Kirk, S. A., and J. J., McCarthy, *The Illinois Test of Psycholinguistic Abilities*. Champaign, Ill.: University of Illinois Press, 1961.

obvious and less complex procedures for training pertinent for the most common difficulties encountered with such children. Such techniques are being developed and tested and appear in the literature. The knowledge needed by the teacher for this purpose would appear to be available.[4]

Since learning disorders are so widespread in the pupil population, every classroom teacher will come in contact with these problems. Therefore, education is needed throughout the classroom teacher population. Although teacher training institutions can be requested to provide such information for new teachers, the same information is required by already practicing teachers. There is, therefore, a need for in-service training programs and institutes which will provide such information to all teaching personnel. Not only is there need for initial information but, because the field of learning disorders is developing rapidly (as is every other field of education), there is a need for a continuing in-service education program to keep teachers abreast of the latest developments in their profession.

With such upgrading of professional skills among teachers, a large number of children with learning disorders can be handled adequately within the regular classroom environment. It is desirable that they be handled in this manner since their problems do not set them off from their peers sufficiently to warrant more drastic procedures. Furthermore, such retention within the classroom maintains the basic relationship to education represented by

---

[4] Frostig, M., and D. Horne, *The Frostig Program for the Development of Visual Perception.* Chicago: Follett Publishing Co., 1964; Kephart, N. C., *The Slow Learner in the Classroom.* Columbus: Chas. E. Merrill, 1960; Cruikshank, W. A., *A Training Method for Hyperactive Children.* Syracuse: Syracuse University Press, 1961; Johnson, D. J., and H. R. Myklebust, *Learning Disabilities: Educational Principles and Practices.* New York: Grune and Stratton, 1967; Strauss, A. A., and L. E., Lehtinen, *Psychopathology and Education of the Brain Injured Child.* New York: Grune and Stratton, 1947.

these difficulties and encourages an attack upon them which is educationally based.

Clinical Procedures. A second group of children have problems that are somewhat more extensive or which somewhat more intensively interfere with processes considered important in the classroom. Such children tend to fall increasingly behind in classroom activities. Their difficulties are frequently severe in the tool skills and hence they consistently interfere with a large number of presentations. The result is that such children slip further and further behind unless they receive special attention for their specific problems. This gradual loss of achievement is disturbing to the child and further interferes with his progress. He, therefore, tends to display an increase in problems as time goes on.

Such children would appear to profit from an intensive but limited therapeutic attack upon their specific problems. Such an attack can best be provided through a clinical approach. The model for such a program could well be the speech correction program provided by many school systems. In such a program the child is removed from the classroom for scheduled periods of therapy in small groups or in individual contacts with the therapist. At the end of the therapeutic session, he returns to his classroom.

For these moderately severe problems, such a facility seems desirable. Because of their evident difficulty in the classroom and their own awareness of this difficulty, the effect of stigma attached to special attention to problems is reduced so that their difficulties are not magnified by special treatment. At the same time, they learn so much from association with their peers and from the bulk of classroom presentations that it is not feasible to remove them permanently from the classroom environment. The short term, intensive treatment period can frequently relieve their problem sufficiently to permit them to once again keep up with their class.

A number of systems have instituted such clinical facilities, either directly in relation to the classroom program or in specialized clinical services such as pupil personnel services or psychological clinics. In some cases, community clinics or hospital clinical facilities have been used. Case records indicate that in many such children an intensive clinical attack can alleviate the problem sufficiently in a limited period of time to permit the child to achieve in the classroom situation.

Such clinical approaches should be educational in nature. Many of these children have other problems in addition to their learning difficulties. Thus, emotional problems are very frequent within this group. Many such emotional problems are the result of the failure in achievement. It is felt that the clinical program advocated for the school should be primarily a learning clinic and should concern itself primarily with the learning problem of the child. If other problems exist, they should be treated in facilities appropriate for the nature of the problem. Such additional treatment can occur simultaneously with or apart from the treatment of the learning disorder. Although cooperation between these agencies is essential, it is thought that the learning clinic should limit, as far as possible, its efforts to the treatment of the learning problem.

Such a clinical facility requires the services of an individual skilled in the diagnosis and treatment of learning disorders. It is felt that this individual should be basically a teacher and that his basic background should be education. The specific skills and knowledge required to deal with the special problems of these children should be added to a foundation of preparation in the field of education. Such an individual should become a clinical teacher. His primary function should be to remediate learning problems so that the child can achieve within the framework of the educational system in the customary classroom situation.

It seems desirable to maintain the administrative tie of such special teaching with the elementary supervision group. The most successful examples of clinical teaching appear to be those in which this function was retained in elementary supervision and the clinical teacher remained administratively responsible to this supervision. Since the treatment is designed to be limited although intensive, it seems better to maintain the child in the stream of the regular educational process rather than to interrupt this progression by assigning him for a limited period to a special facility not directly responsible to the overall educational procedures.

Special Classes. There will remain in the school system a number of children whose interference with learning is so extensive that normal classroom procedures are largely impossible for them. Furthermore, this interference is so intensive that it seems probable that these children will require specialized educational presentations for the rest of their school experience or at least for a major portion of it. These "hard core cases" have little to gain from normal classroom experiences since these presentations are so confusing to them that they intensify rather than reduce their problems.

For such children, the special room seems appropriate. In such a room, specialized learning situations are presented and intensive attacks are made upon the learning disability. Frequently, educational aims and objectives with respect to curriculum need to be revised in view of the probable limited attainment of basic skills by this group.

This last group of children would appear to fit the requirements of the customary special education category. The customary procedure of a special room where this group is segregated from their peers for intensive specialized treatment for relatively long periods of time seems appropriate.

Such special classes, however, should be kept flexible. Where changes in learning ability occur, provision should be made for transfer of the child into one of the other facilities for dealing with his learning disability. Every effort should be made to return him, whenever possible, to the main stream of education.

Procedures

Therapeutic. Primary attention has been given in the literature to the development of therapeutic procedures for dealing with the learning disorders of children. Such procedures attempt to alleviate the interference with the learning process so that the child can learn from more normal presentations such as those of the classroom. Through such therapy the child's overall problem is reduced. Most clinical procedures as well as the teaching principles discussed earlier in the present volume have had therapeutic results as their aim.

Obviously, the direct approach to the problem is through such therapy. With any child, a careful initial diagnosis should be made and all possible remedial measures should be attempted.

Prosthetic. In some cases, however, due either to the nature of the interference or to the limited extent of our therapeutic knowledge, such remediation cannot be achieved. In still other cases, although remediation may ultimately be achieved, therapy will need to extend over a long period of time. In the meantime, the child may drop further and further behind and this continued failure may result in an intensification of his initial problems.

In such cases, prosthetic techniques may be useful. An attempt is made to give the child a technique which will permit him to perform even though the normal processes for such performance are disrupted. He is provided with a learning "crutch" as it were, which although it contributes little to the solution of his basic problem, permits him to perform with a certain degree of success.

When a child who has difficulty with ocular control is allowed to point with his finger or is given a pointer to help him keep his place, a prosthetic procedure is being used. Color coding and similar devices to help structure the material on the page for the child are also prosthetic devices. In the behavior area, the use of isolation booths to reduce distractors serves the same purpose.

Such prosthetic devices are extremely useful since the child is required by the demands of the culture to progress in learning over time. Whenever therapy will be prolonged so that it will not be able to keep pace with this requirement, the use of a prosthetic device, if possible, is indicated. It should be remembered that such devices do not represent a "cure" and are not designed to attack the basic problem. They are only designed to permit the child to keep up, as nearly as possible, with the demands of the environment while a more basic attack on his problems is being carried out. As such, they should be considered temporary procedures which will be eliminated as soon as the therapeutic procedures have become sufficiently effective. In the meantime, however, they serve a very important purpose.

Curricular. Normally one sense avenue plays the dominant role in the organization of psychological material. This dominant sense is relied upon for the major portion of the information upon the basis of which the child solves his problems. Other sense avenues contribute information which is correlated with that of the dominant sense but it is the latter which provides the basis for the overall organization of material. The contribution of the other sense avenues is largely confirmatory or supplementary. The child can, therefore, be expected to learn most easily and to absorb information most efficiently when it is presented through his dominant sense avenue. Although this dominant role is usually taken by the visual sense, there are a significant proportion of children in whom some other sense is more important. Thus, there are a large number of children for whom audition is dominant and who learn most readily from auditory presentations. Still other children rely on tactual and kinesthetic information and learn most easily when they manipulate material. For this latter group, concrete presentations which can be maneuvered provide the best source of learning.

In the normal child the differences between the sense avenues are relatively slight and these children learn with approximately the same ease regardless of the presentation. Information is related and interrelated for them and they translate from one sense presentation to another with ease. In the child with learning disabilities, however, these differences between sense avenues are apt to be much more marked. This child may find it extremely difficult to process information which is presented through a sense avenue which, for him, is not intact. On the other hand, he may find information presented through his more intact sense avenue relatively easy to work with. It should be emphasized that these differences are related to the processing of information within the central system and not to the operation of the sense organ itself. The intact sense may not be the most acute sense. However, even though information may be harder to garner through this sense, its processing, after it has been received, is much more efficient. The result is that this sense avenue is much more efficient for learning even though its external function may be limited.

Such disparity between the perceptual processing of various types of sensory information makes it desirable to present, in the classroom situation, the basic information to be learned in more than one way. The same information should be presented wherever possible through each of the three most frequently utilized sense avenues. Thus, the child whose primary sense avenue is vision can obtain the information visually which another child, whose primary sense avenue is auditory is obtaining through an auditory presentation. If multiple presentations are made available, the child can choose that one which, for him, is most efficient.

An example of such multiple presentations is provided by a classroom of fourth-grade children. The unit for study was archaeology. One group of children was studying this subject through textbook and encyclopedia materials augmented by pictures and filmstrips. A second group was studying the same basic materials through audiotapes which discussed archaeological subjects. Supplementary filmstrips to accompany the tapes were available which the child could use if he found them helpful or omit if he found them confusing. Still a third group of children were working with archaeological artifacts, some of which were original and some of which were reproductions obtained through the local museum. Information gathered through manipulation of these objects could be augmented through either tapes or filmstrips if the child desired. These three types of learning situation were available simultaneously within this single classroom. Any given child could select the type of presentation which he found most efficient. The teacher circulated from group to group seeing to it that the basic information of the unit was being learned by whatever procedure was used by the child.

In this classroom, a single unit of information was being taught through three major sources of learning. Multimedia presentations and audio-visual materials have been in use for a long time. In most cases, however, these additional materials have been used as auxillary sources of information, the basic core of the lesson being carried by the customary textbook presentation. Where there is conflict or lack of correlation between sense avenues, however, these additional sources need to be thought of as the basic presentation of the information. For such a child, the primary source of information may well need to differ from that of the customary presentation. Thus, for him, the audio-visual material must become, not an auxillary source, but the primary source of information. Further, his most efficient presentation should be made available to him consistently, not sporadically as audio-visual or similar materials happen to become available or convenient.

Much experimentation is needed to determine the most efficient means of making available information contained in typical classroom units of study through different sense avenues. Most of the investigations to date have concentrated on the development of supplementary materials designed to augment the typical presentation. For the child with learning disorders, however, these materials need to be designed as primary sources of information. Typical classroom presentations will vary from subject to subject. For some, visual presentations are standard, for others auditory presentations are used while for still others, such as scientific experiments, the basic presentation is manipulatory. If the child has one or more sense avenues in which learning is inefficient, he is bound to be in trouble somewhere. Because of the great disparity between his sense avenues, this difficulty is frequently magnified until it results in academic failure or lowered achievement. Such failure could frequently be minimized if consistent learning presentations were made available through his most efficient perceptual avenue.

For such a purpose, classroom presentations need to be much more flexible than is currently the rule. Not only must a much wider range of materials be made available but it must be recognized that not all children in the class need to have the same routine. Children should be permitted freedom to use those materials which are most adequate for them. The material to be learned will thus become the determining factor in classroom procedure not the method by which it is learned. For the normal child, such freedom of learning method will increase learning efficiency. For the child with learning disorders, it may well spell the difference between success and failure.